TRISPECTIVE
THE 3-N-1 QU

American Quilter's Society
www.AmericanQuilter.com

The American Quilter's Society or AQS is dedicated to quilting excellence. AQS promotes the triumphs of today's quilter, while remaining dedicated to the quilting tradition. AQS believes in the promotion of this art and craft through AQS Publishing and AQS QuiltWeek®.

DIRECTOR OF PUBLICATIONS: KIMBERLY HOLLAND TETREV
ASSISTANT EDITOR: ADRIANA FITCH
CONTENT/TECHNICAL EDITOR: CAITLIN M. TETREV
PROJECT EDITOR: SARAH BOZONE
GRAPHIC DESIGN/TECHNICAL ADVISOR: CHRIS GILBERT
COVER DESIGN: MICHAEL BUCKINGHAM
QUILT PHOTOGRAPHY: CHARLES R. LYNCH

Additional copies of this book may be ordered from the American Quilter's Society, PO Box 3290, Paducah, KY 42002-3290, or online at www.Shop-AQS.com.

American Quilter's Society
www.AmericanQuilter.com

LIBRARY OF CONGRESS CATALOGING-IN-PUBLICATION DATA PENDING

This painting is "The Creation of Adam"...

...and this shows only a small section of it...

This was painted around 1512...

...by an artist named Michelangelo...

This painting can still be seen today...

...on the ceiling of the Sistine Chapel in Rome.

Adam's finger and God's finger are not touching...

...because God and man are not on the same level.

God's right arm is outstretched to impart...

...the spark of life from His own finger into Adam's...

On this pose Adam's arm mirrors God's...

...to remind us that we are created in God's image.

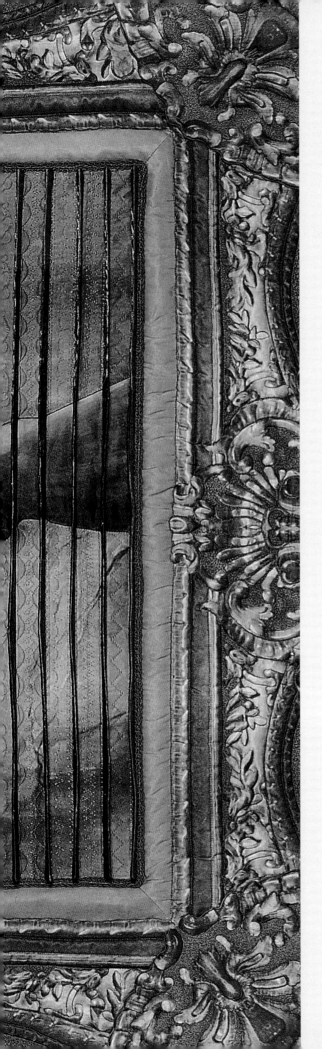

Dedication and Acknowledgments

So many people have made a difference in my
pursuit of this endeavor.

The following are only a few of the people to
whom I would like to say MANY THANKS:

My husband Henry who endured countless nuked meals and
watched trails of dust bunnies
scamper around while these quilts were being made;

Marc Montgomery whose computer genius
skills helped make this 3-N-1 quilt design possible,
not only for me to make these quilts, but also to
share these instructions with others;

The "Three Little Crowes," who allowed me to use their
photos in one of the quilts, my brother Carey and his two
sons Brian and David. Thanks also to Sharon Crowe;

Mischele Hart who is herself an inspiring quilter,
yet always lauds the talents of others;

The Blue Ridge Quilt Guild for its uncountable
challenges and fabulous quilters, who always choose to be
supportive friends instead of competitors;

Teresa Smith and her entire Bernina In Stitches
staff for their continued tolerance of my
multitudinous questions about stitches;

Jim Sledge whose photography has made my
work shine with JOYful brightness;

Kimberly Tetrev who has been a patient and fabulous editor;

The entire staff of the American Quilter's Society
for their hard work in providing so many venues
and services that inspire all quilters.

Contents

Preface: Anatomy of a 3-N-1 Quilt

If you've never walked past a 3-N-1 quilt before, then you haven't experienced the magic of seeing the images change from one person (or scene)... to another... and then to another... while you take just a few steps. The first response from most first-time viewers is, "What's happening? This is cool!" Once you understand the structure of this quilt, you'll be in on one of the best-kept secrets in the quilting world. This "secret" is summarized below. It all begins with three of your favorite photos, such as three of my family members (father/two sons) shown in Figure 1a. You will then manipulate those three photos in your computer (or get a friend to do it for you) to make a file that will look like the one in Figure 1b. You will print this new design onto fabric, then stitch and/or embellish its columns as much as you wish while that piece is flat. Finally you'll sew it into pleats (referred to as "the pleated section" throughout this book). It will look like Figure 1c.

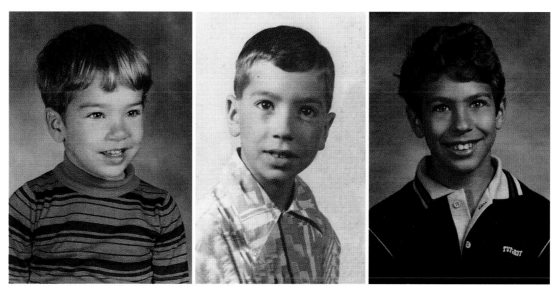

Figure 1a.

Figure 1b.

You can give the pleated section a simple edge finish, mount it inside an actual wooden frame, or stitch it into an elaborate fabric frame. With the latter, it could look like Figure 1d.

Figure 1c.

Below is what viewers would see inside the frame if they stood at the left.

Below is what viewers would see inside the frame if they stood at the right.

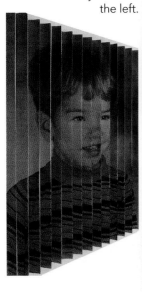

Figure 1d.

If you make a 3-N-1 quilt, then viewers will walk by and say, "What is happening? This is so cool!" You'll know that the images aren't changing—just the perspective of the viewers as they see the three different images. But, sh-h-h-h-h-h! That's our secret!

Chapter 1

What You Should Know Before You Start Your First 3-N-1 Quilt

Inspiration comes to all of us when we least expect it. Several years ago I was sitting in my car waiting for the traffic light to turn green, when a large revolving billboard with triangular panels caught my attention. The panels rotated every 10 seconds from one image, to another image, to a third image, then it started all over again. This process intrigued me, and as I tried to sleep that night, a quilt that changed images began formulating in my mind. It took several years for me to work through *how* this concept could be transformed into fabric, and after many attempts with numerous samples, a finished quilt finally emerged. After that, my quilting life changed forever. The journey has been quite thrilling, and I'm hoping *you* can join in the fun.

The purpose of this book is to share the complete process with you to make a 3-N-1 quilt. First a disclaimer: We often hear advertisements for ideas that are "Quick and Easy," but for the sake of honesty, I must communicate that making this quilt will be neither quick nor easy. Some moderate quilting or sewing experience will be needed. It will, however, be worth the effort, and the process can be immensely exciting! One of the early steps will involve the use of a computer and a photo-editing software program. In Chapters 2-4 there are carefully illustrated instructions. People who are acquainted with photo-editing program can typically zip right through them. However, read on to the special notes section if you want to avoid using a computer at all.

> ### Quilter's Note 1:
> The majority of quilters would rather "stitch" than deal with a computer. If you are not computer-savvy, consider asking a computer friend to prepare your image file. Simply select your three photos and let your friend follow the instructions in Chapters 2-4.

> ### Quilter's Note 2:
> If you want to begin with the actual stitching of a quilt (instead of preparing your own design), go directly to www.storytellingworld.com for information on how to order your choice of any of the designs that have already been prepared for this unique quilt style. Type 57870 in the white rectangle for Handout Codes (and click on submit), then go to Chapter 5 to proceed with the quilt construction. Consider starting with a smaller sample for your first experience, then let nothing hold you back!

A Sneak Peek!

Demonstration Quilts

The step-by-step explanation for this process is described through three separate quilts that were prepared just for this project. One is small and relatively simple, another is larger and intentionally has several more complex (but optional) features, and the third is much smaller and showcases people. The illustrations and explanations in this book will relate to these three quilts.

For all three of the demonstration quilts used in this book, there are three downloadable complimentary image files available for anyone who would like to practice these same techniques before tinkering with their own new files. For information on obtaining these files, see Quilter's Note 2 above.

Demonstration Quilt 1: Magical Toys

The first quilt is small (23" x 22") with very few stitches and embellishments. Figure 2a shows the images used for this first demonstration quilt, and Figure 2b shows the completed quilt.

The steps for the quilt below are purely fun and energizing. The pleat columns are ¾" in height, and the frame is sweet and simple. Complimentary files are provided for you to work along and practice creating this exact same quilt file if you wish. (See the Quilter's Note 2 for the web link). Ready-to-stitch fabric for this quilt is also available on the same link.

Figure 2a.

Figure 2b.

Special Note:

The above images are credited to Ukrainian artists Anya Stasenko and Slava Leontyev, who have kindly given me permission to use these images for this project. You may also download these three complimentary files. See Quilter's Note 2.

Demonstration Quilt 2: Sleep, Pray, Scream

This second demonstration quilt features three of the world's most famous art pieces. My husband and I have been very fortunate to have traveled to a variety of interesting art galleries and historic art sites. We have seen all three of the art pieces selected for this second 3-N-1 demonstration quilt. When I first saw *Starry Night* by Vincent van Gogh at the Museum of Modern Art, I immediately wanted to stitch it. The swirls, stars, and shadows of buildings and other structures just begged to be explored with thread. Viewing *The Creation of Adam* by Michelangelo on the ceiling of the Sistine Chapel in Rome was a compelling experience, although in a very different and reverent way. Seeing *The Scream* by Edvard Munch at the National Gallery in Oslo was also a mesmerizing experience.

Figure 2c shows the three images used for Sleep, Pray, Scream, and Figure 2d offers a tiny glance at those three views of the completed quilt.

Larger images of these paintings and completed quilts are shown elsewhere in this book. As with the Magical Toys quilt, complimentary images for Sleep, Pray, Scream are also available for potential practice.

Figure 2c.

Figure 2d.

Demonstration Quilt 3: THREE LITTLE CROWES

The third demonstration quilt (7" x 10") features people. Figure 2e shows the three photographs used, and Figure 2f is the finished quilt. (See Chapter 12 for the framing.)

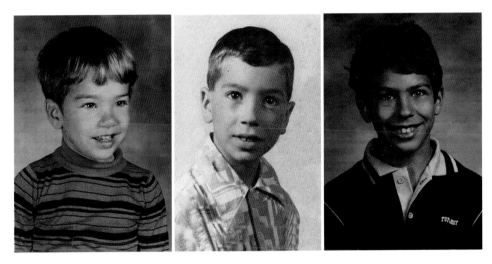

Figure 2e.

Figure 2f.

A sneak-peek summary of the steps in the 3-N-1 quilt process:

A. Select and tweak three photos that you want to feature.

B. Prepare these three photos in one file for printing onto fabric.

C. Decide whether or not to frame the quilt and if so, select the framing choice you would like.

D. Stitch and quilt the sections, then combine the different pieces.

Chapter 2

Selecting and Tweaking Your Photos

The first step in making a 3-N-1 wall quilt is to select three images you would like to feature. The possibilities are endless, and you can have great fun with this decision. For example, think about the following:

❖ A photograph of you, one of your mom, and one of your daughter.

❖ Your father, husband, and son.

❖ You (now), you (in college), and you (as a child).

❖ Three grandchildren (or nieces/nephews/cousins/aunts/friends/co-workers, etc.).

❖ A friend/family member at three different stages of life.

❖ Three pets.

❖ Three photos you made during three trips (or three pictures during the same trip).

❖ Three houses you've lived in (or churches/schools you attended).

❖ Three meaningful photos of the bride or groom (as a wedding present).

❖ The same tree/flower/scene during three different seasons.

The list is endless. Once you start thinking about this, you will realize that you could make so many different wall quilts. Have fun with your photo selection. The information in this chapter can help you in this decision-making process.

You will need to have Adobe® Photoshop® ready before proceeding with the next steps.

Factors in Photo Selection

Here are some factors to consider when you are choosing photos for a 3-N-1 wall quilt:

❖ Select images that are approximately the same width/height/orientation or ones that could be easily adjusted/cropped so they could be modified to be the same size without looking distorted. For example, if you are selecting scenes, you wouldn't want a very long image of a wide mountain range matched with another photo of a single tall tree. These would be difficult to merge into the same project.

❖ Choose photos that have at least a moderate contrast in color or value.

❖ Regarding people, if you're flipping through a drawer full of photos, and you encounter an 8" x 10" of your sister, a 4" x 6" of yourself, and a wallet size of your mom, don't despair. It is likely that these can be easily adjusted to be the same approximate size. A later section will demonstrate that.

❖ Also for people we have found that head shots turn out so much better than photos where there are lots of busy surroundings or where the head size is very small.

Figure 3a shows two images that would *not* work very well in a 3-N-1 wall quilt because of the difficulty in recognizing those pictured and because of the lack of details or a busy background. If these same photos are examined in an album, they of course have great interest, but when transferred to fabric and separated into small columns, they would have unappealing results. The people would be very difficult to recognize in photos like these, especially if the head photo is split into two different columns.

Figure 3a.

Tweaking Your Selected Photos:

After deciding upon which three photos you want to use, you are ready to modify them for your first 3-N-1 style wall quilt. Decide which one of the three images you would like to be visible to viewers when they are standing at the left of your quilt. Do the same for the right and the center. Name these three files. Scan these three selected images into any photo-editing software program, and for the sake of convenience, consider naming the files "RIGHT.jpg," "LEFT.jpg," and "CENTER.jpg." (Later you'll be glad these are their file names.) Set each of the three images to a resolution of 150. Now you are ready to adjust the images for height and width.

Select the Image Height:

Decide on a desired photo height that will best fit all three images. If one is considerably taller than the other two, for example, do some cropping at this point. Continue tweaking until all three images are the *exact* same height. The number of height inches won't matter at all (as long as all three images are the *same* height). Be sure to use the "Constrain Proportions" tab when making height adjustments on each individual image.

Determine Your Desired Column Width:

If you have very small images (around 10" in height), a ½" column width, works nicely. Medium sizes are great with a ¾" column width and larger images can use 1" column widths.

Determine the Image Width:

Continue with your cropping and changing image size functions until the *left* and *right* images are exactly the same width. This width should be evenly divisible by your chosen column width. If your chosen column width will be 1", then your width for all three images should be an even number of inches. The center image will be 1" narrower than the right and left images, since there is one extra pleat for the right/left photos. The same principle applies to the ¾" and ½" column widths. More details are provided in later sections.

Initial and Tweaked Images for Demonstration Quilt 1 (Objects): MAGICAL TOYS

Figure 3b shows the images of the three photos selected for the first demonstration quilt.

Figure 3b.

The three original images shown in Figure 3b above are *almost* perfect for this project. They have beautiful color and contrast, and they are approximately the same size. However, they do need a bit of tweaking and cropping. Here are some suggested steps for this process:

❖ Begin with the center image and crop both the left and right sides. If the height is satisfactory, just leave it alone. Set the width to a number evenly divisible by your selected column width.

❖ Open the remaining two images and adjust their height to match that of the center image.

❖ Set the width of the right and left images to the same width as the center image **plus one exact column-width extra** that you have chosen for the inset of your wall quilt. For example if you selected 1" column widths, then make the right and left images 1" wider than the center image. If you want column widths of ¾", then make the right and left images ¾" wider. To illustrate, if the width of the center image is 12" and the desired column width is 1", then the right and left images would each be 13" wide. The height for all three images should always be the same.

Figure 3c shows all three of these images after they have been adjusted. Perfect!

Figure 3c.

Initial and Tweaked Images for Demonstration Quilt 2 (Scenes): SLEEP, PRAY, SCREAM

Figure 3d shows the three original images used for the second demonstration quilt.

Figure 3d.

As you can see, there are many more adjustments needed in order for these three paintings to be in the same quilt, but I was determined to make it work. I must admit that did spend several hours in Adobe® Photoshop® trying to adjust them so they looked professional. *Starry Night* had a landscape orientation, while *The Scream* had a portrait orientation. The section of *The Creation of Adam* was between the other two. Finally, however, adjustments were made so that all three of these paintings looked great together.

Figure 3e shows the three final tweaked photos. As you can see, the biggest adjustment was with *The Scream*. I decreased the portion of the sky area and I gradually resized the image from top to bottom. I continued with this tweaking until I was happy with the outcome. The final size for the right and left images was 29" wide and 24" high. The center image was 28" x 24" (1" narrower because I used 1" columns for this piece and the center image always needs to be one column's width narrower than the right and left images).

Figure 3e.

Initial and Tweaked Images for Demonstration Quilt 3 (People): THREE LITTLE CROWES

Figure 3f shows the original three photos selected to demonstrate the third quilt.

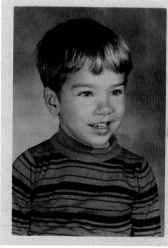 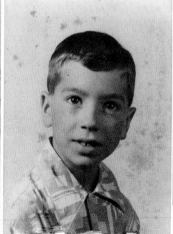 

Figure 3f.

Human faces are fun to do! Below are the tweaked photos of my brother (center) flanked by his two sons (all taken when they were about the same age). I had to remove the border from the left photo, then I photoshopped the shirt bottom of the center photo and cropped it. Finally I cropped/resized the left photo. Figure 3g shows the results of all the photo-editing.

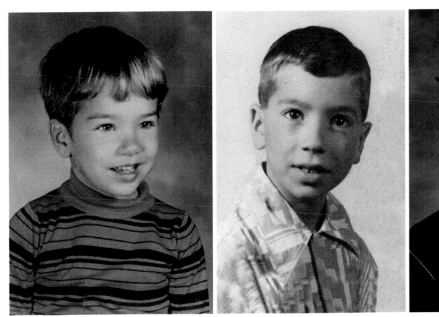

Figure 3g.

Chapter Summary
Select three photos you want viewers to see in your quilt. Tweak them in a photo editing program until all three photos are the same height. The widths will be the same for the two outer (right/left) photos, and the center photo will be a column's-width narrower. Set all three images to a resolution of 150.

Chapter 3

Preparing Photos to Print onto Fabric

After tweaking the three photo files according to the description in Chapter 2, you will further tweak them into one master file for later printing onto fabric. This chapter explains this procedure for preparing master files with half-inch, three-fourths-inch, and one-inch columns.

Making 1" Column Files (using Adobe® Photoshop®):
MAGICAL TOYS

Make a blank document in a photo-editing software program that will be the exact width and height of the image sections when they are all flat. For example, if the width for the Left/Center/Right are 14"+13"+14", then the new master document width will be 41". The height will be the one you've set for all three of the designated images. Set this new file at a resolution of 150.

Name this file to indicate a new project, such as MagicalToysMASTER.jpg. This file will be referred to in this document as the master file (because it will have the three photos, etc.). Your new screen will look something like Figure 4a.

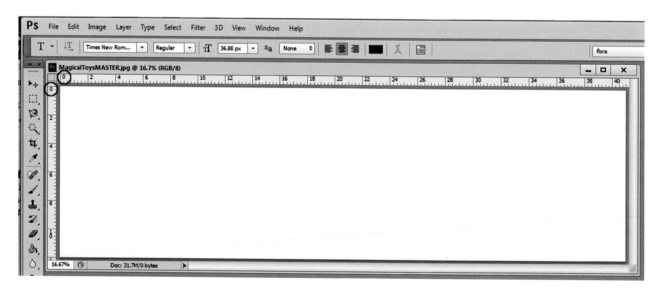

Figure 4a.

In Figure 4a you can see the parameters for both the height and the width of the file that will contain the columns from all three of your tweaked images. This file is the one that will later be printed onto fabric, so you want to take special care to prepare it the way you want it to eventually look.

For your final image to be as professional and "clean" as possible. The next step is very important. **Enlarge the master file to 200%** so the ruler grids can easily be seen and the inch mark indicators will be very wide. Use your cursor to pull the file so the **zero** for the width and the **zero** for the height are both in the upper left corner of the ruler grids. Figure 4b shows how your new screen will now appear.

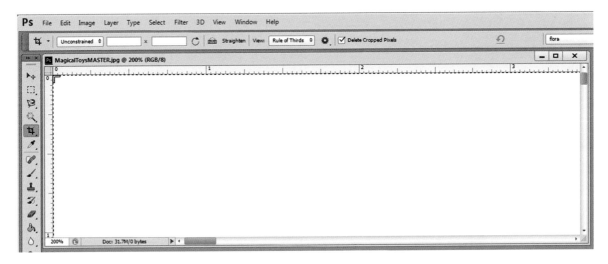

Figure 4b.

Notice how much larger the inches now appear on the ruler grids. (This 200% enlargement is the only difference in Figures 4a and 4b.) This zoomed view will be extremely helpful as you proceed.

Now open **all three** image files that you have prepared for this project. **Rename each one**. I added an x at the end of each file name: "LEFTx," "RIGHTx," and "CENTERx." By renaming these three files and working with them, you will prevent the possible loss of your original designs if you accidentally goof during the next steps. Figure 4c shows these three renamed images for the quilt MAGICAL TOYS. If you have downloaded these same images (see Quilter's Note 2 on page 10), you may use them to follow along with the steps for preparing 1" columns.

Figure 4c.

Align these three images on your screen so you can see the top bar of all three of them. **Important: Enlarge all three of these images to 200%.** This may change the positions of the ruler grids, so scroll over until the left side is on zero for the width for all three images. I leave the horizontal area near the middle because the details of the image can be seen (instead of seeing just the top border areas, which sometimes seem to all look alike).

Figure 4d is an approximation of what your new screen might look like for the quilt MAGICAL TOYS.

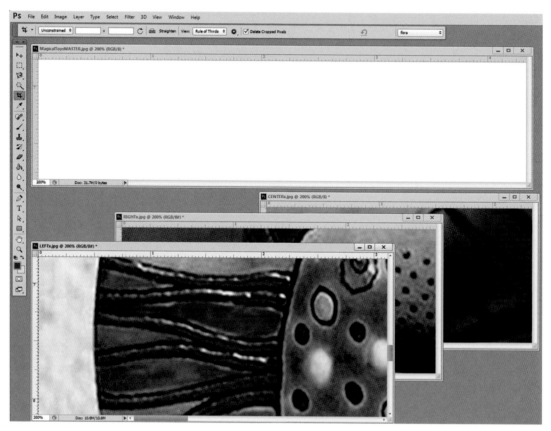

Figure 4d.

Notice the Following About the Above:

❖ The three images are intentionally stacked. Such a screen arrangement will be of tremendous help during the next few steps.

❖ The order of the three images is as follows: left, right, and center. This is the order you'll be using, so having the three files already in this order on your screen will be easier. Note: It may logically seem that the order should be left, center, right, but trust me, it isn't.

❖ The three images may appear "fuzzy." This is because of the zoom, but that doesn't mean they will be fuzzy later. Not to worry.

You are now ready to begin designing the actual fabric that will later result in the pleated portion of your 3-N-1 wall quilt! Here are the steps:

❖ If your software program has a "snap-to" function, set it to be operational.

❖ Begin with the LEFTx.jpg file. While that image is selected, click on the rectangular marquee tool. This marquee icon can appear in different places on computer screens, depending upon which version of Adobe® Photoshop® is being used (or if the tool bars have been moved). On my screen it is the second icon in the left column, and it resembles a dotted square). This icon looks like the one shown in Figure 4e.

❖ When you left-click on this marquee icon, the top toolbar will change to the features offered for this function. On that toolbar, click on **Style**, then choose **Fixed Size**, and type in **1 in** to indicate that's the **Width** you want your columns to be, then type in the **Height** in the choice to the right. Your **Height** selection will be the exact height of all three of your images. The three images I'm using for this explanation all have a height of **12 in** as seen in Figure 4f.

❖ With your LEFTx.jpg image selected, position the cursor (which now looks like a crosshair) **absolutely exactly** on the "0" inch line at the extreme left of the design and then left-click. The marquee tool is activated, so this will automatically outline a full 1" column (although you'll see only a portion of it), and you will see the dotted line outlining the one-inch section. This should occur automatically each time after the style/size has been set. Figure 4g is an illustration of how this dotted section should appear.

Figure 4e.

Figure 4f.

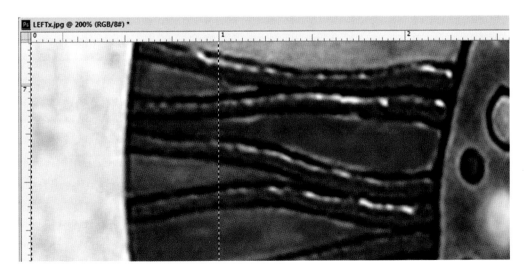

Figure 4g.

Can you see the dotted lines at the right and left of this one-inch column in the LEFTx.jpg file? Notice also how **exact** these dotted lines are directly on both the **zero** and the **one-inch** lines. This is what you will strive for during the tagging of each of these columns. Remember that you aren't viewing the full column during this process and you are seeing only the middle portions of the images, but it isn't necessary to see the full image—just the ruler lines. I always pull the images up to approximately the middle so I'm not dealing with the top borders, which tend to look the same in so many cases.

❖ Now go to **Edit** and **Cut** (type **Ctrl+X** for Windows users) while these dotted lines are showing. This will temporarily **Delete** that 1" column, but don't worry because this is not your original file—just a copy to use for the purpose of designing the fabric. You will want these columns to disappear (by deleting them) from your temporary files as you work through this process.

❖ Now select the **Master File** (and double check to make sure you have the zoom to 200%). Position your cursor on the exact "zero" ruler line at the farthest left spot possible. Now go to **Edit** and **Paste** (**Ctrl+V**). This will **Paste** the one-inch column from your LEFTx.jpg file into the master file. Step one has been accomplished! Your computer screen will look like Figure 4h.

Figure 4h.

The one-inch column from LEFTx.jpg has now been moved from that file and placed into the MASTER.jpg file. The next step will be to do this same thing with the right image.

Select the RIGHTx.jpg file. You will repeat the first step you did with the LEFTx.jpg file by doing the following:

❖ Left-click on marquee (if it isn't already activated).

❖ Position your cursor exactly on **zero**.

❖ Left-click to see a new bounding box.

❖ Hit **Ctrl then X** (or go to **Edit** and **Cut**).

❖ Return to the MASTER.jpg file.

❖ Position your cursor on the 1" mark.

❖ Left-click to see a new bounding box.

❖ Hit **Ctrl then V** (or **Edit** and **Paste**) to drop the new 1" column from the Right file into the Master file.

Your screen will now look like Figure 4i.

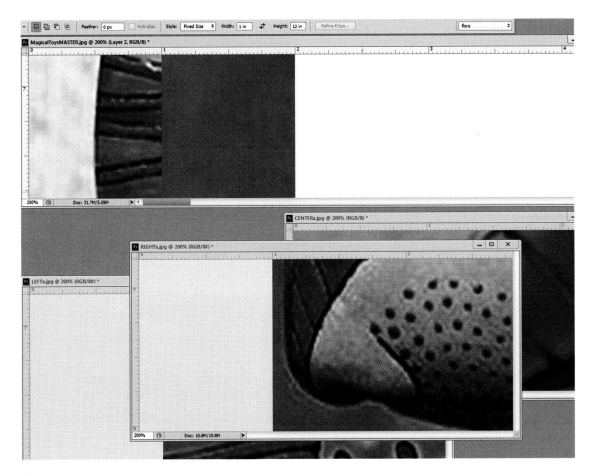

Figure 4i.

Notice that the second image is in the forefront at this point. By observing which of the three images is actually in the foreground, you can't get off track regarding the order of the upcoming columns. Simply click on the next one in the line of three (from left to right).

❖ It's now time to transfer the first column from the center into the master file. Do the same as above, but when you get to the MASTER.jpg file **left-click** your cursor on the **2" mark**. Type **Ctrl then V** to drop the new one-inch column from the CENTER.jpg file into the MASTER.jpg file. Your screen will now look like Figure 4j.

Figure 4j.

You now have the first three 1" columns lifted from each of the three independent files and dropped into the MASTER.jpg file. You will continue with the second inch of each of the three files and essentially do the same thing. In case you have wondered why we have been deleting (**Ctrl then X**) each time, now you know. When you return to each file, you will begin at the exact point where you see a portion of the image. The portions you have already pasted can no longer be seen, thus you can't accidentally tag them again (causing duplicates and messing up the master grid). In this manner there will be no need to "remember" where you were the last time that file was open, and the process is much smoother. Note that as you proceed through deleting the 1" columns from the three independent files and dropping them into the MASTER.jpg file, you will frequently need to use the bottom scroll on each file to "scoot" or drag the file image to the left so you can continue to see the remaining portions of the non-transferred columns.

Until this process has become second-nature to you (and it will!), here is what you will continue to do:

- ❖ Select the LEFTx.jpg file.
- ❖ Position the cursor on the exact edge of the portion of the image that is currently showing.
- ❖ Left-click.
- ❖ Type **Ctrl then X**. (Make sure you don't accidentally type **Ctrl then C** for "copy"!)
- ❖ Go to the master file.
- ❖ Position the cursor on the exact spot where the next column should be placed.
- ❖ Left-click.
- ❖ Type **Ctrl then V**.

Repeat the above steps with the RIGHTx.jpg file.

Repeat the above steps with the CENTERx.jpg file.

Continue until all of the columns have been transferred to the MASTER.jpg file. At this point, your MASTER.jpg file will look something like Figure 4k.

Figure 4k.

After you finish with the last column of the last file, you may then delete the three "XFiles." (Forgive me, I just couldn't resist this pun.)

For an Image Border:

It will be helpful to add a border around this image because you will need a seam allowance on the edges. To do this while your file is on your computer screen, go to **Image**, then to **Canvas Size**. Click on **Relative**, then type the numeral 1 in both the width and the height (thus giving a ½" border on all four sides). For the Canvas Extension Color, identify a shade you want the outside border to be. Consider choosing a shade closest to the dominant color in your three images. Click **OK**. Figure 4l shows one possible image.

Figure 4l.

Making One-Inch Column Files (Adobe® Photoshop®):
SLEEP, PRAY, SCREAM

Figure 4m shows the three photos of the paintings used for Demonstration Quilt 2.

Figure 4m.

This second quilt that is used for illustrations in this document is more elaborate in its stitching, quilting and framing. It is prepared with one-inch columns, and it is considerably larger. The exact same steps will be followed for these three photos, except the width and length of the master file will be larger. Pull the three provided complimentary images to practice making this file if you wish (see Quilter's Note on page 10). Figure 4n shows what this master file looks like.

Figure 4n.

Making ¾" Column Files (Adobe® Photoshop®):
MAGICAL TOYS

It is likely that most of the 3-N-1 projects you make will have either 1" or ¾" columns. The process for the ¾" columns is identical to those explained for the 1", except that you will make every column with a width of ¾" instead of a full inch. The only difference in what you set on the Adobe® Photoshop® screen will be the width of .75". See that detail circled in red in Figure 4o. Your columns should automatically snap to ¾".

Figure 4o.

Figure 4p shows what the file would look like for the MAGICAL TOYS quilt with ¾" columns.

Figure 4p.

The dimensions for the above are 42" x 12.75" (including the border area, which was a ½" on all four sides).

The math method for ¾" marking: You might think that any column width that was not a whole number would involve lots of math. It can, if you wish. For example, you would need to make sure that your image heights were identical (no "math" needed here), then you want the width of your left and right images to be one of the following inch measurements: .75, 1.5, 2.25, 3, 3.75, 4.50, 5.25, 6, 6.75, 7.50, 8.25, 9, 9.75, 10.50, 11.25, 12, 12.75, 13.50, 14.25, 15, 15.75, 16.50, 17.25, 18, 18.75, 19.50, 20.25, 21... (each time, just add ¾" or .75 to the previous number). For your center image, simply subtract ¾" from the width that you chose for your left and right images.

The non-math method for marking non-inch segments: This is fairly simple. You will once again make your images the same height, and you would simply allow a tidbit of extraneous background/edging to be at the right of all three images. This will result in about a fraction of an inch at the right of each photo remaining after you have filled in the master file as you wish, but at least you will not have needed to measure. For the purpose of providing as much different information as possible in this document, this ¾" width has been stitched on the quilt MAGICAL TOYS. All illustrations on the following pages for that quilt will have the ¾" columns (as shown in Figure 4p). All illustrations for SLEEP, PRAY, SCREAM will have the one-inch columns.

Making ½" Column Files (Adobe® Photoshop®):
THREE LITTLE CROWES

For 3-N-1 wall quilts that are in the range of 10.5 inches in height, ½" columns can be a good choice. The process for designing ½" columns is identical to those explained for the one-inch, except that you will make every column with a width of ½" instead of a full inch. The only difference in what you set on the Photoshop screen will be the width of .5 in. See that detail circled in red in Figure 4q. Your columns should automatically snap to ½". The THREE LITTLE CROWES quilt has been used to demonstrate ½" columns.

Style: Fixed Size   Width: 0.5 in   ⇄   Height: 12 in

Figure 4q.

Figure 4r is a reminder of how three prepared 7" x 10" images look.

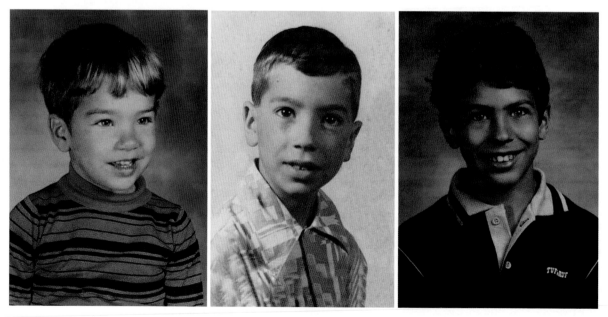

Figure 4r.

Figure 4s shows how the completed master file might look for the above images.

Figure 4s.

An Alternative: The Quick "Raw-Edge" Method (With No Computer Photo-Dissection)

The above procedure for the image preparation is the standard for this quilt concept. Because it takes some time with the steps, some quilters might seek an easier or quicker method that does not involve dissecting photos in a photo-editing software program. This alternative choice will not look as professional, but it will work nicely for small gifts or early practice. For this method, you need to adjust the photo size to a maximum of 10.5" in height for all three images. If you do not mind doing horizontal piecing of the image sections, any height will work. Purchase 1+ packs of iron-on inkjet fabric sheets (any brand). After you have tweaked your three images to the same height and the same widths for the two outer fabrics (and 1" narrower for the center), print each of these images as whole images onto the purchased iron-on fabric sheets. Then cut each image into 1" columns. Iron them alternately onto a full backing, being sure the columns are butted together smoothly (edge-to-edge). Trim the backing, leaving about an inch around all edges. Use an overlapping stitch to secure each of the raw-edge columns. Proceed with decorative stitching and finishing as described in later sections. Note that any column width other than 1" could also work.

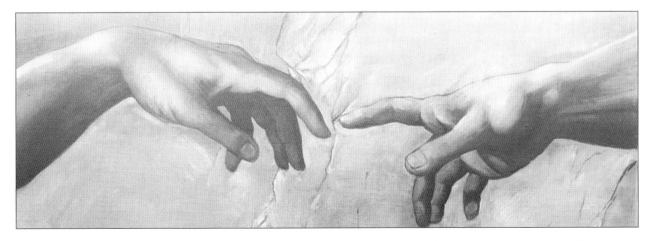

Chapter 4

Printing Your Prepared Photos onto Fabric

Now that your image is prepared, you are ready for it to be printed onto fabric. There are several ways this can be accomplished.

Using your home computer: It is possible to divide your prepared columned image file into sections and then print them with an inkjet printer. If you do, be sure to allow extra for seam allowances at the right/left edges, and keep in mind that your project will be bulkier in the places where sections are stitched together. Be sure to check your printer's manual to determine the types of ink suggested for fabric.

Recommended method using commercial companies that print fabric: There are several commercial companies that print fabric for quilters, garment makers, etc. I have had great success with Spoonflower. Here are the steps to accomplish this:

❖ If you have not ordered from Spoonflower before, then go to www.spoonflower.com and click on **Join** near the top. At this point you can either upload your prepared design or create an account.

❖ After logging in click on **Create**, then click on **Custom Fabric** in the drop-down menu. You will upload your file by following the steps on the screen. Note that their maximum file size is 40MB. If your file is larger than this do another Save As in your computer and reduce the file size until it is under 40MB.

❖ Choose your type of fabric. The "Basic Combed Cotton" works nicely, or you can request the "Basic Cotton Ultra" which makes the colors a little brighter.

❖ Select the amount of fabric to order. Make sure you order enough to fit the entire image on the fabric. You will be able to see the image on the screen before placing your order. To make sure you are ordering yardage, click on the down arrow (to the right of the words "Fat Quarter") and then click on the word Yards. Now click on the needed quantity in the "QTY" box to the left of the word yards.

❖ Click on "add to cart" via the gold rectangle below the price.

❖ Enter your shipping address and other details. Under **Connect**, you can email a customer service agent at Spoonflower if you have any problems or use their **chat** option during normal working hours.

❖ The shipping time is typically 8-10 days.

Chapter 5

Preparing the Fabric for Stitching

After prepared images are printed on the fabric:

❖ Press out any wrinkles, being careful not to stretch the fabric, in any direction.

❖ Place two layers of heavy cut-away stabilizer on the back of the printed image fabric. Batting is not needed for this section. Extend the stabilizer around all four sides by at least a ½". Lightly spray baste these three layers together to secure them—making sure to get the image fabric adhered to the stabilizer in all areas for non-cotton fabrics. For cotton or other sturdy fabrics, a light spray will suffice.

Side Notes/Tips:

❖ Regarding the stabilizer choices, there are many different kinds. I typically use two layers of heavyweight cut-away stabilizer or a light/medium layer and one heavy layer if my top fabric is relatively sturdy or if the image area is small. You can make other stabilizer choices depending upon the thickness and sturdiness of your printed fabric. On a practice sample, experiment with different stabilizer layers and thicknesses until you discover a perfect one for your project.

❖ Don't even think about using some of your "ugly fabrics" to serve as a stabilizer for this pleated section! Although it won't be seen (and you'll be getting rid of it), it will fail to serve a very important function. Commercial stabilizers are **thin** but **stiff**, and they do not have a grain of fabric—three features that are needed for this project.

❖ Currently, there are several different color choices of stabilizers. You can't go wrong with white (or sometimes beige). If you decide to use bobbin work in the columns (explained in a later section), then don't choose black.

❖ When you use a spray adhesive to secure the focus fabric to the stabilizer, carefully position the inch columns so they are **exactly straight**. You might have to move the fabric a bit if the design is not printed exactly straight on the fabric. If the piece you are stitching isn't straight, then your final design columns won't be straight either. This is the time to be "perfect" regarding this alignment.

Stitching the "Peak Lines"

The next step is to stitch at the "peak lines" that will eventually become the top points of the future pleats. To accomplish this, follow these steps:

❖ Straight-stitch exactly down the center line of each column that will later be the "peak" in the final wall quilt—but not down any of the other column lines. If it gets confusing regarding which column lines to stitch, make marks in the upper seam allowance before you start the stitching process. Those can be seen in Figure 5a.

❖ Begin stitching at least a ½" above the image section (inside the seam allowance area) and extend the stitching through the end of each column (again, inside the seam allowance area). This continued stitching keeps the threads in the actual images from loosening as you work with the fabric.

❖ This "peak line" stitching will occur in every third column, and it will appear as if you have "stitched in the ditch" even though there are no seams. At this point it is extremely important to stitch in a straight line and to start with the correct column line (where the right and left images join). This column stitching serves several purposes, primarily to dictate the later fold line. Obviously, a crooked stitch line will encourage a crooked fold later. Figure 5a shows some completed peak line stitching.

Figure 5a.

For additional support and stabilization, stitch two extra columns, one about a ¼" from the far left image edge and another from the far right image edge (both are in the margin). These two extra stitched lines will make life easier for you during the remaining stitching by not allowing the final columns to move around and become crooked.

After finishing all the checked columns, trim the thread tails, leaving them about an inch long so the seam won't begin to loosen. (These threads will be tucked under and hidden later.)

Side Notes/Tips:

❖ Keep in mind this may be very slow stitching because you don't want to be off by even a "thread's worth," and you want your stitching to be very straight. You have likely heard quilt teachers say, "Don't watch the needle, but look ahead…." However, in this case, do watch the needle.

❖ Notice that the red checks at the top of each to-be-stitched column indicate which lines to stitch (in case you get distracted).

❖ A walking foot is a great choice for stitching these straight lines. Another good choice is a dual feed foot with an open toe area for better visibility. I use either Bernina's Foot 20D or my walking foot for these column stitches.

❖ If your three merged images have identical colors at any of these peak lines, use an erasable pen to mark the straight lines—in advance—to insure that the stitch line is exactly straight.

❖ Be sure to start at the same side (at the top or the bottom) each time you stitch a new row, in order to prevent possible distortion. It will be very tempting to stitch to the bottom of the first row, then turn slightly and stitch from the bottom of the second row to the top. Don't yield to temptation on this matter.

❖ Make every attempt to get the needle position exactly "in the ditch" for every stitch—a tedious task for some, but it will be worth it later.

❖ This column stitching gives an additional stabilizing effect that will be helpful throughout the remaining steps because it prevents the fabric from scooching around. It also provides a very helpful visual starting/stopping point for some later stitching inside the columns.

❖ Regarding the thread color for stitching these column lines, try to match thread colors whenever possible. Some people choose invisible thread, but be very cautious with later ironings if you do. Others choose a neutral beige/gray. For MAGICAL TOYS, I selected Isacord Poly Thread #0722 (Khaki) for the top thread, and The Bottom Line #654 (Oatmeal) in the bobbin.

Because it will be a while before you actually fold this entire section into pleats, feel free to fold one or two of them just to get a "sneak peek" of what this might look like later. (Use an iron, an art burnisher, or just finger-press it.) Obviously, you'll want to unfold it before proceeding.

Chapter 6

Stitching Inside the Columns: Some Quick Choices

Now that the fabric and its underlying layers have been stabilized, decisions need to be made for the stitches inside the columns. The sky is the limit regarding these choices. The choices can be no stitching (the pleats will be sewn together later), simple free-motion stitching, or machine-based decorative stitching. This chapter offers several suggestions, so you can make any number of additional choices.

No Stitching

When considering the kinds of stitches to select for these long narrow columns, keep in mind that there is the choice of no stitching. These long, narrow columns will "stand up" in the later pleats without extra stitching, if that's what you want. This could even be the method you choose for your first 3-N-1 wall quilts (especially, if there are people in your selected images). On the other hand, if you would like a more embellished quilt (or if you plan to enter your piece in a quilt show), you might want to proceed with other choices. The remainder of this section will describe some of these choices.

Special Notes for Column Stitching

The information in this section uses two very different demonstration quilts, MAGICAL TOYS, and SLEEP, PRAY, SCREAM to illustrate a variety of unusual techniques and choices for column stitching. Although your own quilts will be different, examine these chapters for ideas concerning the choices regarding how your personal 3-N-1 wall quilt might be stitched or embellished. By reading through the stitch choices and the procedures, you will have gained an abundance of information before you begin your own unique quilt.

The following suggestion applies to *all* of the illustrated column stitch choices: If you are stitching any "running" stitch (decorative, free motion, etc.), continue stitching off the bottom and top columns into the seam allowance (at least a half-inch). In most cases this can keep you from tying off thread tails later. It can result in a more polished final look. While you are stitching this section, the top and bottom edges might appear unsightly (as shown in Figure 6a), but later they will look very smooth. Notice also how stitching off the edge allows you to travel from one column to another without cutting the thread. Don't be distressed at the unsightliness of the long bottom and top edges. It will magically become beautiful later.

Figure 6a.

Another helpful thing to remember is that the two ends of your fabric sandwich will *roll together* very easily and nicely. This makes your fabric easier to maneuver on a domestic sewing machine. See this demonstrated in Figure 6b.

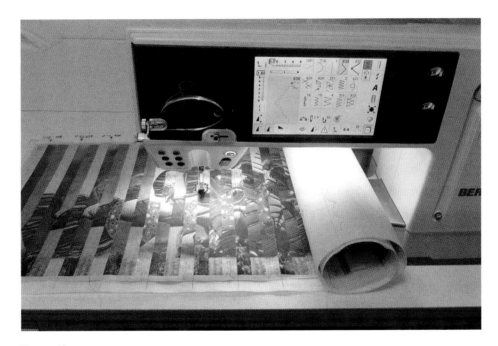

Figure 6b.

Think Before You Stitch

Before making decisions regarding which types of column stitches you want to do, first decide what mood you want to create with your stitches. These decisions will help you get much closer to making smart column-stitch choices. For example, my stitch-appearance goals for SLEEP, PRAY, SCREAM were as follows (with the more prominent ones in bold):

For *Starry Night*: **uneven, jagged, irregular,** chaotic, bold, swirling, bumpy, rough, unbalanced, craggy, fitful, sprawling, loud, in-your-face.

For *The Creation of Adam*: **reverent, humble, unobtrusive,** reserved, subdued, pale, inconspicuous, tasteful, unnoticeable, modest, quiet.

For *The Scream*: **depressing, bleak, dismal,** daunting, funeral, hopeless, sad, joyless, mournful, somber, gloomy, and dispiriting.

With the majority of the above descriptors relating to "non-straight" stitches, one might think that this sewing process would be easy, but it wasn't for me. After years and years of attempting to master straight and even stitches, suddenly I was trying to achieve an uneven or chaotic stitch. This was very difficult! It seems that I had to practice more for these stitches than I had when I was learning to do straight stitches. I began by exploring some of the easier and quicker ones. However for the majority of the columns, I decided to tackle some more intricate ones that typically take longer. First, let's look at a few of the faster ones:

Free-motion quilting in these columns is a great choice, and it can be relatively quick, depending upon how skilled you are with this type of stitching. It can also be fun to stitch, and your quilting can either follow the pattern designated in your images or it can simply meander. Figures 6c, 6d, and 6e show some samples from SLEEP, PRAY, SCREAM.

Figure 6c.

Figure 6d.

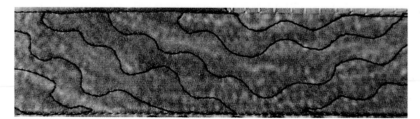

Figure 6e.

Thread painting can also enhance these narrow columns. Figure 6f shows very light and loose thread painting for the tree bark in Magical Toys (after the columns were flattened). The thread choice can make a great difference for any type of thread painting. Mettler Polysheen Embroidery Thread Color-#9979 Salt-N-Pepper (black and white variegated with a short return) for this tree stump was perfect.

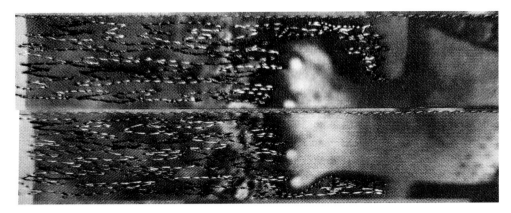

Figure 6f.

Stippling is another quick and common stitching technique. Figure 6g is a sample of a very loosely stippled section (photographed after the columns were flattened).

Figure 6g.

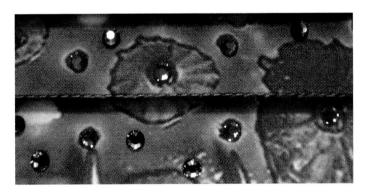

Figure 6h.

Beads, crystals, and buttons can also decorate these columns (although, technically, crystals are not stitched). Most beads and buttons would need to be stitched by hand, but all three of these can certainly help embellish the columns. Figure 6h shows columns prepared with crystals (photographed after the columns were flattened). Be very cautious with using anything that would prohibit the ironing/pressing of the columns after the pleated insert is finished. The items can sometimes puncture through a layer that is ironed on top of it. Pressing the columns flat is a beneficial step, but if there were shank buttons or other 3-D items, this step could be more difficult. Crystals could be adhered after this pressing is done, but buttons would be more problematic unless they could be discreetly glued.

Keep in mind that practicing on a sample piece can be of great benefit. The following chapters offer some detailed choices.

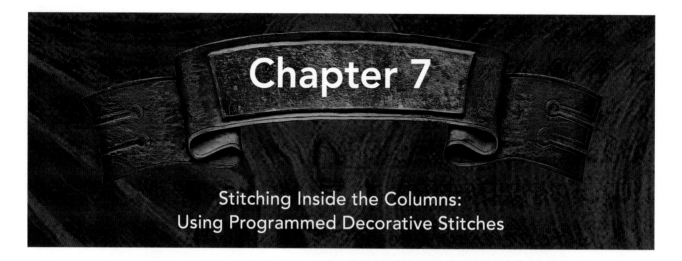

Chapter 7

Stitching Inside the Columns: Using Programmed Decorative Stitches

The majority of stitching inside the columns will likely relate directly to the actual fabric design. For outer areas and generic backgrounds, though, the decorative stitches that are pre-programmed in your machine can do the job nicely. The choices for decorative stitches are limited only to those programmed in your sewing machine(s) and to your ability to do variations of them by altering the stitch width and length. Below are some suggestions:

❖ Select the decorative stitches to be sewn down each column. Make a plan for how these stitches will be sequenced.

❖ Draw columns on a practice sample (with the same stabilizing layers that your actual quilt will have). Stitch a few inches of the decorative stitches you have chosen. Write the number of each stitch. Make note of any changes in width or length that you make. Figure 7a shows four examples.

(**Note:** These illustrations below are actual rough scans of my own samples. They demonstrate that such practice samples do not need to look perfect; they are merely a record of needed information about these non-straight stitch patterns. The long solid lines show the one-inch markings, but the illustrations on this page are not to scale.)

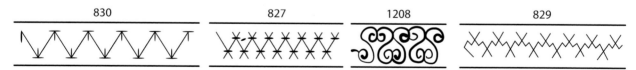

Figure 7a.

❖ By doing the practice samples, you will know **where** to begin the stitching in the column. The needle for some decorative stitches will penetrate the fabric at the far left when the stitch begins, while others will start at the center or at the right. Knowing this in advance will make a big difference when you use these stitches on your "real" project. It is very tough to remove decorative stitches, especially those that are dense. Practicing on separate fabric sandwiches will help eliminate the need to do so.

❖ In some cases a double run works nicely for very narrow decorative stitches. Figure 7b shows three examples of these. While you are stitching some practice samples, be sure and mark where one of the presser foot toes would be positioned for the beginning of the stitching. The elongated "C" shapes on the right of each sample stitch (for both Figures 7a and 7b) indicate where the left presser foot toe should be placed. Save your samples for future reference.

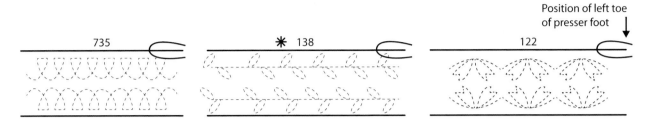

Figure 7b.

❖ Closely examine the pattern of the stitch to see if it moves either sideways or backwards as it stitches. Determine if your column can accommodate this stitch as you are sewing.

❖ Select one of your decorative stitches and decide where to begin stitching in the column. If you will be stitching the entire column, begin outside the image in the seam allowance area (so you will have a very smooth entry without obvious stopping/starting points). Leave the thread tails on both ends.

❖ Decide on the thread color. Do you want the thread to blend in very subtly or do you want it to stand out? Select accordingly.

❖ If a decorative stitch has a specific directionality (such as the two examples shown in Figure 7c), you might choose to flip the stitch pattern horizontally before you begin stitching the opposite side of the same column. Look at the two examples from SLEEP, PRAY, SCREAM. These decorative stitches would need to be flipped when the fabric sandwich is turned around and stitched from the opposite side of the arm if you want the stitches to have the same pattern orientation.

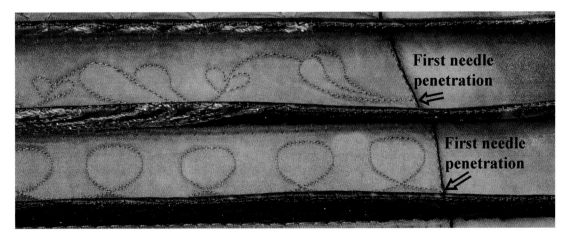

Figure 7c.

❖ If you are stitching partial columns, consider beginning at an obvious starting point inside the column rather than at the top or the bottom of the column and then stitching toward a design change. The examples in Figure 7c also demonstrate this. By beginning inside the column at the start of the decorative motif, an incomplete stitching of the motif can be avoided. Each one of the two stitch patterns was begun exactly at the triple-stitched seam of Adam's arm. They then continued toward the top or bottom of the image section. Otherwise the leaf and/or the row of circles could have reached the arm in the middle of the motif, thus leaving an awkward and incomplete connection/ending. Also, the initial needle penetrations for the two samples in Figure 7c do not begin their first stitch in the center of the column (where we typically begin.) Instead, the stitches will begin at the far right. Once again, stitching a sample in advance will allow you to determine these starting points and avoid possible mistakes.

Side Notes/Tips:

❖ You will need to be very attentive during this entire decorative stitching process. Sometimes simply glancing away can throw off the direction of the stitch, and catastrophe can happen in a nanosecond. Also, the stitching can sometimes go astray. If you're paying close attention, you can stop the machine and decide how to remedy any problem that might occur.

❖ If the stitching extends through the top or bottom of the column, always stitch off the image and into the seam allowance.

❖ When you begin the decorative stitch inside the column (rather than at the top or bottom), bring the bobbin thread up to the top before stitching. This can avoid numerous undesired thread entanglements. Pull through enough thread tails so you can later thread them into a hand needle and tie them off on the back side.

❖ As an alternative to burying the thread tails, you can "stitch in place" 3-4 stitches in the same spot at the first stitch in the decorative pattern. Then begin the decorative stitch and later cut the earlier thread tails very close on the quilt's surface. This may not look as professional, but if you take the time to trim it carefully, it will work.

❖ It is smart to use the machine's hand-wheel to insert the needle into the first stitch of the decorative design (unless you are beginning in an outer seam allowance). It is amazing how many times I thought the first stitch would occur slightly to the right/left/top/bottom from where it should have begun. This manual guidance can ensure the decorative stitch will at least begin where it should.

❖ Consider saving the extreme right and left double columns to stitch last, then select your most attractive decorative stitches for those two columns (because these stitches might be viewed the most).

❖ I begin each row of these decorative stitches with my foot pedal. After the design has gotten to a good beginning, I use the auto-stitch button to stitch the remainder of the row on slow speed.

❖ Stay attuned to the amount of bobbin thread you have remaining. For the majority of decorative stitches, if the bobbin runs out while stitching a long row, it is almost impossible to start up again and have a smooth appearance at the point where the bobbin was replaced.

❖ Each time you finish a row of decorative stitches and change to a different stitch for a new column, pull your practice sandwich out again and practice one or two motifs of the new stitch before continuing with the "real" quilt. You'll be glad you did.

❖ I chose Isacord Poly Thread #1172 (Ivory) for the beige areas on the SLEEP, PRAY, SCREAM quilt. The shade blends with the background fabric. For MAGICAL TOYS, I selected a different shade for each of the three images: Isacord #0722 (Kahki) for the center columns, Isacord #1172 (Ivory) for the left, and Isacord #5664 (Willow) for the right and Mettler #9979 (Salt N Pepper—a black and white variegated with a short return) for the tree stump on which the critter is sitting. I love the way this thread looks like tree bark!

❖ Remember that all machines are different. Your machine will have an entirely different set of these special stitches than the ones shown here. (Those shown in this document are the resident stitches in my Bernina 830.) Explore what your machine will do, and have fun with this process. It is amazing what an adjustment in either width or height can accomplish! Keep a folder of your all your stitch samples for future reference. Sometimes we think we can remember the numbers, but soon we forget. Remember also to jot down any stitch adjustments you have made for the effect you want.

❖ If you are one who gets easily distracted or visually confused, you might want to plan and number your chosen stitches for each column. Figure 7d shows how I outlined the stitches for MAGICAL TOYS. I began with all of the rows for the left image, and I stitched those first—only in the background and not inside the critter. I did all of these columns of stitches first because I could keep the same top thread in the machine. Then I planned the stitches for the right image (see Figure 7e), and I stitched those column background sections. I ended with the center images (see Figure 7f). I marked these three sections one at a time, and I used different colors of markers. This kept me from being confused while I had the complete wad of fabric in my machine.

The above is only a tiny beginning for what can be accomplished with decorative stitches. Have fun exploring the possibilities with your machine.

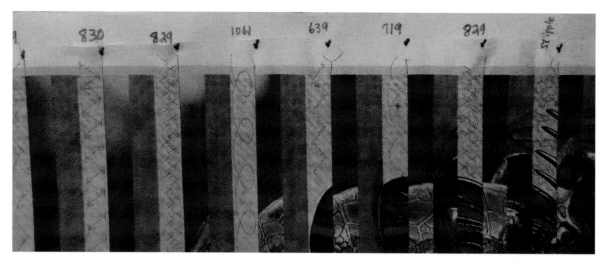

Figure 7d.

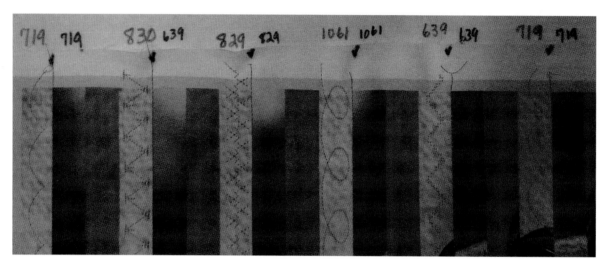

Figure 7e.

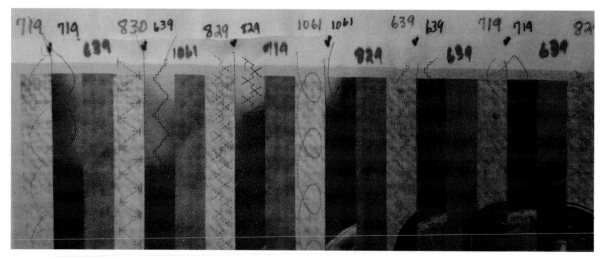

Figure 7f.

Chapter 8

Stitching Inside the Columns:
Bobbin Work

An interesting and effective alternative to decorative stitches, thread painting, etc., in these columns is bobbin work. For this type of sewing, thick thread is hand-wound for the bobbin, and the quilt is flipped over so the right side is facing down and the back side is facing up. Swirls or non-defined fabric patterns are typically good choices for bobbin work. Here are the directions for bobbin work in the 3-N-1 quilt columns:

❖ Hand-wind a bobbin with a thicker thread of choice. This selected thread will be one that is too thick to go through the top needle, but it should be one that you just love and one that can enhance your project.

❖ Adjust the tension. Each machine is different. I use the bobbin adjuster and set back the bobbin tension on my Bernina 830 by moving the second white dot two notches to the left.

❖ Insert the bobbin. Note that inserting a hand-wound bobbin will differ from one machine to another. I insert the bobbin, pull the thread through the clip, and pull it toward the thread cutter, but I don't use the thread cutter. Let the end of the thread dangle loosely in the bobbin area. Now close the bobbin door.

❖ Use a matching color for the top thread (typically 40 weight).

❖ Select an appropriate presser foot. I use Bernina's foot #20 because it has an open toe area that allows better stitch visibility. Use whichever foot is applicable for the stitching you'll be doing.

❖ Lower the feed dogs.

❖ Bring the bobbin thread to the top by turning the hand wheel. Pull out a few inches of this thick bobbin thread, then hold onto it before beginning to stitch.

❖ Flip the quilt so the back side is up, and position it for stitching.

❖ As you are sewing, pay close attention to the signal that the bobbin thread may be running low. When that signal first appears, just go ahead and assume it will stitch only a few more inches and then stop and wind another bobbin.

❖ After completing all the bobbin work, return the changed settings back to normal.

Side Notes/Tips:

❖ There are numerous magazine articles, online videos, etc., that offer information about bobbin work.

❖ When hand-winding your bobbins, make sure the direction of the thread is the orientation needed for your specific machine. Some machines vary with regard to this direction, so explore this first.

The above explanation of bobbin work applies to a generic or meandering stitch that does not follow any pattern in the designs of the images. You simply stitch in the column in whatever manner you wish. If you do want to follow any lines in the image, however, you won't be able to see them from the back, so you won't know where to stitch. There are two ways to overcome this problem:

One: Use a light box or tape your fabric layers onto a window you can see through. Draw lines where you want to sew. If you have the two layers of white stabilizer, there should be no problem seeing the design through both layers. This will give you the visual information you need to stitch on the back side while you have heavy thread in the bobbin.

Two: This method is more complex, but it allows you to see very intricate details of the image. In your computer open the file of the original image you want to use for the bobbin work. Rename the file with the word *mirror* added, and save the new file. In your photo-editing software, flip the mirror image icon horizontally to actually obtain a mirror image. In SLEEP, PRAY, SCREAM, I used bobbin work only for the *Starry Night* image. Figures 8a shows the "before" (regular) image, and Figure 8b shows the "after" (mirrored) image.

Figure 8a. Regular Image   Figure 8b. Mirrored Image

Print the mirrored image onto fabric, and iron on a fusible web onto the back of it. Remove the paper section from the ironed-on fusible web, and carefully cut this new fabric into the exact column widths of your project. (For example, if your master file consists of 1" columns, cut this fabric into 1" strips. If it is ¾" columns, cut the mirrored fabric into ¾" strips, etc.) Position each cut strip in its precise mirrored position on the back of your fabric sandwich. Figure 8c is a photo of how a portion of this looks with these strips ironed onto the back. *Note that the photo for Figure 8c was taken after the stitching was finished for the other two images, which is why those background stitches are noticeable.*

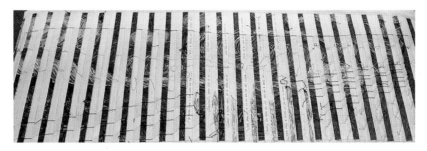

Figure 8c.

With this method you can see all the details of the original image, and you can stitch up a storm wherever you would like. Figure 8d shows a section of this bobbin work on the front side after this quilt was finished and the columns were flattened to show *Starry Night*.

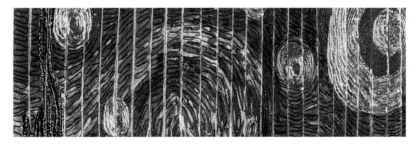

Figure 8d.

The design of *Starry Night* has lots of winding swirls, and it begged to have these thick stitches on the top of the quilt. Because thick thread can't go through the upper needle, bobbin work was a perfect choice of stitching for this design.

The thread choices for bobbin work will greatly alter the appearance of your final project. Experiment with a variety of threads before deciding which ones to use (although that can result in a lot of bobbin-winding).

Side Notes/Tips:

❖ For the orange portions of the moon/stars, I wound Ricky Tims' Razzle Dazzle Thread #271 by Superior on my bobbin. I wound Wonderfil Dazzle Metallic Rayon Thread #DZ 2000 for the white/silver sections, and Wonderfil Sizzle SX11 Gold for the blue areas. I stitched these in gentle waves so that the front sides would flow with the natural patterning of the painting.

Chapter 9

Stitching Inside the Columns: Words

In addition to the choices explained in the previous chapters, keep in mind that words, phrases, and/or sentences may also be stitched in these columns. The selected words may be anything you feel will help provide adequate information for your quilt. They may be stitched in free-motion style, or the resident stitches in the sewing machine may be used, or the words may be created in embroidery software. Figure 9a shows the explanation of *The Creation of Adam* in six sentences—separated by the fingers that almost touch. The words in Figure 9b identify the artist for *Starry Night*, and those in Figure 9c reveal the price paid for one of Munch's versions of *The Scream*.

Figure 9a.

Figure 9b.

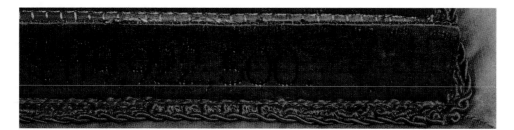

Figure 9c.

The 3-N-1 wall quilt title or the name of the quilter or other pertinent information may also be used—as could any other words, phrases, or sentences that seem appropriate for the project. Such text could add fun to the quilt by enticing viewers to make new discoveries.

Quilts that include people could have text with the names of the individuals along with other information such as year of the photo, age of the person at the time the photo was made, etc.

Side Notes/Tips:

❖ The actual sentences used in the section for The Creation of Adam are:
(1) This painting is "The Creation of Adam" ... this shows only a small section of it.

(2) This was painted around 1512 ... by an artist named Michelangelo.

(3) This painting can still be seen today ... in the ceiling of the Sistine Chapel in Rome.

(4) Adam's finger and God's finger are not touching ... because God and man are not on the same level.

(5) God's right arm is outstretched to impart ... the spark of life from His own finger into Adam's.

(6) In this pose Adam's arm mirrors God's ... to remind us that we are created in God's image."

The above sentences were selected for the purpose of giving a concise background of the painting, especially for the purpose of communicating that this section is only a small part of the complete painting on the Sistine Chapel.

❖ The sentence used for *The Scream* was, "Edvard Munch painted four versions of *The Scream* in 1893. In 2012 one of them sold for $199,922,500."

❖ For *Starry Night*, the title was stitched on the left side, and "by Vincent van Gogh in 1889" on the right side.

❖ Any words may be stitched into these columns, just don't overdo it or it may appear to be an "assignment."

Chapter 10

Stitching Inside the Columns: Special Effects

Occasionally there will be areas in the images that could be enhanced with special effects. Study the subplots of your selected photos to see what seems to invite some bedazzling stitching.

Special Stitching in *Starry Night* Columns

In this painting the cypress trees seemed to jump right out of the fabric and request festive treatment. I decided to try the following technique with this section: Wind about 15 strands of thick decorative threads in a length that is slightly more than double the area to be covered. Tape the thread ends together, as shown in Figure 10a.

Figure 10a.

Fold this entire group of threads in half, and position the looped end at the top of one of the tree positions, as shown in Figure 10b.

Figure 10b.

Notice in Figure 10b that a straight pin is holding the looped threads at the top end. Stitch over these threads just enough to hold them firmly in place inside the narrow column. Figure 10c shows samples of two sections after all threads have been positioned and stitched.

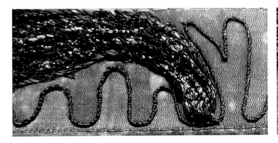 

Figure 10c.

Figure 10d shows a larger (flattened) 6-column section of a completed cypress tree (turned sideways) using this technique.

Figure 10d.

Side Notes/Tips:

The threads I used for the cypress tree are:
- ❖ WonderFil Sizzle 18CY, SM4 (green) [my favorite and the final highlight]
- ❖ Wonderfil Dazzle Metallic Rayon 2854 (green), 100 (green), 7148 (dark blue), 160 (black), and 9000 (black—3 strands at the same time)
- ❖ Mettler No. 3 black; Ricky Tims Razzle Dazzle 254 and 275 (both green)
- ❖ YLI Candlelight Metallic Yarn (green)
- ❖ The top thread for stitching was Isacord 5373 (a deep bluish green)

Special Stitching in *The Scream* Columns
This painting also had several sections that could be enhanced by special stitching. Two of them are discussed and illustrated on the following pages.

The Screamer's Robe: Because the main focal point was the Screamer's head, I wanted his attire to be semi-accentuated. There were many choices for how to accomplish this, and my final decision was to use multiple strands of thick thread to depict his stringy-looking robe. Instead of couching these thread strands, though, I chose to adhere them to their positions inside the narrow columns. Rather than using glue sticks or any type of regular glue, I prepared a template (from poster paper) with a long one-inch opening just large enough to expose the robe area. I reshaped the opening with copy paper whenever it was needed. Then I spray-basted the open areas with the fabric adhesive brand called 505 (although any type of quilt basting spray will suffice). Figure 10e shows a section blocked and being sprayed.

Figure 10e.

Notice how the template (made of white paper) blocked all except the section of fabric that needed the spray.

Next I removed the paper template and positioned thick threads atop the sprayed area, one at a time. The spray adhesive held these threads in place just long enough for later permanent couching.

In these spray-based areas, I positioned either craft thread or Pearl Cotton threads onto the sprayed area, leaving about a ⅟₁₆" section uncovered near the column line where the crease will be later. This adhesive spray is temporary, but it keeps the threads in position for the next step, which is to do free-motion stitching to couch the threads onto the quilt sections permanently. Figure 10f shows the first few threads placed in position to get the section started.

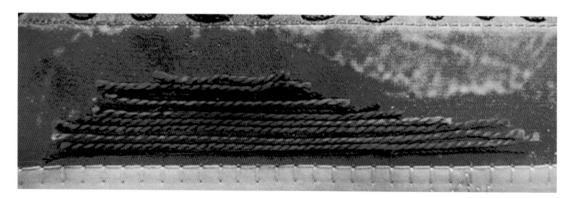

Figure 10f.

In Figure 10f, it may appear that there will be raw thread ends dangling loose and that the final stitching results would be very rough and unsightly. However, additional threads were placed atop these raw ends before the final stitching was completed. By layering the threads in this manner, the bulk of the curve was not a super thick mess of bundled-up, overlapping threads. Figure 10g shows how more threads have been added to cover the raw ends of those earlier shorter threads that were needed to prevent bulk. Notice that the new threads placed atop the earlier ones are looped at the top, and all of these thread beginnings and endings all extend off the bottom edge. All of these loose ends will later be enveloped into the pleat seam and completely hidden.

Figure 10g.

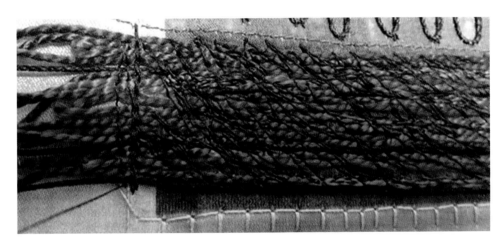

Figure 10h.

Figure 10h shows top-stitching that has been angled in a fashion to permanently hold all of the thick threads in place. This stitching isn't traditional couching, nevertheless it *couches* the threads as needed. This free-motion stitching was angled at about 10 to 15 degrees instead of being exactly vertical. This keeps the threads intact and gives the appearance that the threads (which I did place vertically) are "leaning" slightly to the right. However, I chose to use this couching style because it eliminated the need to bury hundreds of stray thread tails. In Figure 10h, notice that there are now no raw thread tails *inside* the column.

Side Notes/Tips:

❖ Even though I hand-placed the thread strands vertically, after their placement I added 3-4 additional thread strands in the 20-30 degree vertical angle (atop the straight strands). This was an attempt to follow through with the flavor of the original art image. Also, during the free-motion stitching, I adjusted some of the threads so they wouldn't look so uniform. These two combined techniques worked nicely.

❖ Continue with your free-motion stitching until you have achieved the textural look that you like. After you have done enough angular stitching to hold all the threads in the position you want them, then combine the angular and vertical stitching to complete the section. I stitched rather heavily in these areas and at many different angles. (It's a bit like thread painting, and that can greatly modify the look of any design.)

❖ Later after each pleat of the inner portion of the quilt is manually folded, you can look for any additional changes you might want to make, such as adding a couple strands of threads needed in sparse areas. This can be done at the quilter's discretion, but perfection should not be the goal.

❖ The threads I used for this robe were: Laura Wasilowski's Italian Prune, and Burnt Marshmallows, both Size 5. (They can be found at: www.artfabrik.com.) Dark brown thread should be used for both the top and bobbin. I used Isacord Thread #1366 (Mahogany) for the top and Superior Threads The Bottom Line #648 (Dark Brown) for the bobbin. Laura's two thread packs—brilliantly variegated—worked quite nicely for these robe sections, and only a few stray strands were remaining after my practice pieces and quilt sections were completed. The "Italian Prune" thread offered small sections of bright aqua that could also be seen in the original art. During my stitching, I free-motion quilted more of my dark brown top thread on top of the bright aqua threads to slightly mute the brightness of this shade, yet still allow it to do its job. The number of threads you use per column will vary according to the thread choices you make. I used about 15-20 strands for the full column. Experiment with a separate piece of fabric before stitching these columns. Solids give a very different look from those having a color variation. Thread thicknesses numbered higher than a "5" might be difficult to use. Pearl Cotton sizes 3 and 5 are great. Remember that the lower the thread number, the thicker the thread. Look in your craft thread stash for some other possibilities, or use your project as an excuse to buy more thread!

❖ When positioning these threads, leave extensions well past where the netting face pieces will be placed later. (The netting pieces are explained in the following section.) They can be trimmed just before the free-standing face pieces are stitched into the column.

❖ Note that these six sections of extra thread thicknesses will not add to the bulk of the quilting because the threads are **surface** items. The "quilting" will be about the same as the other areas of this large image section. Typically, extra-dense quilting can cause the area to shrink, but that doesn't usually happen in this case.

❖ Remember not to butt these thread strands up to the actual **inside** column lines, but leave a bit of unfilled space. Because these columns will later fold into pleats, it works best if there isn't a dense pile of threads right at the inside column edges. That extra space will not be noticeable when the final folds have been made.

The Screamer's Head: Because the main feature of this painting was the Screamer himself, I decided to treat the stitching on his face a bit differently. After exploring several ideas, I chose to create separate free-standing sections for each column that showed a portion of his face. I used two layers of an extremely thin netting atop a layer of Badge Master, a very thick water-soluble stabilizer that completely disappears in warm water. I traced the six "head sections" and then satin-stitched the borders (changing stitch widths as needed) and used a creative stitch pattern and stippling for the remaining inside head features. Figure 10i shows two examples before they were sewn onto the quilt.

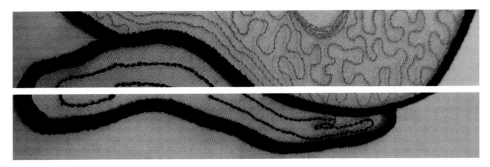

Figure 10i.

After all six sections were prepared, I washed away the Badge Master and trimmed the edges very carefully with tiny applique scissors. I used invisible thread to attach them to the quilt after all other surrounding stitching had been completed. This resulted in a much eerier version of the Screamer than the one in the original painting, and that was an effect I liked. I intentionally avoided any shiny threads or bold colors to accomplish this look, and I selected thread colors that further enhanced this desired eeriness. Figure 10j is a photo of one of the columns after this free-standing netting was stitched onto the column.

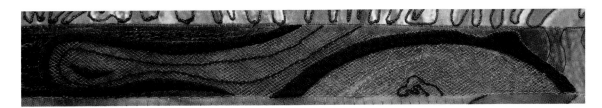

Figure 10j.

Side Notes/Tips:

❖ The satin stitched edges of the Screamer's face served the additional purpose of covering several thread ends of the robe. Therefore, stitching the robe sections first (see explanation on page 52) solved the problem of having visible thread tails of the thick robe threads where the robe and face sections joined.

❖ The thread colors for the Screamer's face (stitched onto netting) were Isacord Thread #0851 (Old Gold) and Isacord Thread #1876 (Chocolate). The bobbin thread matched the top thread in both cases.

Joining the Screamer's Head and Robe: After finishing the pieces for the Screamer's head, set them aside—then stitch the robe threads onto the actual quilt. There will be lots of thread tails from the robe section. Trim those at the bottom of the quilt, leaving about an inch remaining. Working one section at a time, position each head piece over the spot where it will finally be stitched. Peek beneath the head piece and trim the robe thread tails just enough so they will barely be tucked under the head piece after it is stitched on—but not enough for the robe's thread tails to extend and show through the netting.

Side Notes/Tips:

❖ It would be smart to save this step until everything else is completed for this inner quilt section. The less folding and fussing that the netting head pieces receive, the better they will look later. Even though they are relatively strong pieces, they should be handled with care.

Remaining Areas (Many of these were shown in Chapter 6 illustrations):

❖ **For the Sunset:** This area demanded no extra attention, so I sewed rows of stacked, gentle wavy stitches (like packed clouds) from the horizon to the top, in elongated, flattened ovals that seemed to follow the suggested lines of the sky's contours. The top thread color is Isacord Thread #1304 (Red Pepper). For the bobbin in use, any shade that blends either with the orange or other colors in the sunset. Refer to Figure 6d.

❖ **For the Shadows:** This refers to the two walkers on the far left, and the boat/people images. I did a lightning bolt stitch (long, jagged rows of stitches) that merely suggested what was painted. I used Isacord Thread #1366 (Mahagony) on the top and a dark brown in the bobbin. Refer to Figure 6d.

❖ **For the Boards on the Bridge**: I used Stitch #759 in the approximate areas where the slats might join. Calculations aren't necessary here unless you *want* to delve into higher math. To determine where to stitch, I just started with the column at the farthest left and drew straight lines (with an air-erase marker) on the diagonals in the image. After drawing these, I stepped back to see if they looked reasonable. From there, I continued with lines on each of the remaining columns in a manner that would make them appear to be continuous after the final pleats are folded. I used Superior's King Tut variegated thread #981 (Cobra) to create an even more interesting effect.

❖ **For the Fence Rails:** I pulled through crochet thread (Red Heart Brand, Size 3, Dark Brown) into the top and bottom rims of the railings. When I did the free-motion stitching, I began with these threads and did a zigzag stitch (1.5 stitch width/1.5 length) to fasten them in. I then I used the "woodgrain stippling" inside each rail section. (For this I used the free-motion foot #24, with the feed dogs down.) This extra thread thickness positioned on the surface of the fabric gave a nice effect.

❖ **For the Darker Swirls:** I did the same as above, except I did "wavy" stitching in the columns. Again, I used Isacord #1366.

- ❖ **For the Sand-Colored Areas:** In the top, upper center, I followed the swirly lines with straight stitching (Isacord #0722). Any other type of stitch seemed to fight the design and become obtrusive. Even though I had discovered several amazing decorative patterns, it seemed that the viewer's eyes were drawn to the stitches instead of the painting on each of my practice samples—so I went back to the straight or gently curving stitches.

- ❖ **Note:** Scroll back through the Chapter 6 figures and review many of the above suggestions.

Special Stitching in *The Creation of Adam* Columns

This painting was deliberately chosen to be the center image, primarily because it was the one that would receive the least amount of stitching. When the finished quilt is viewed from the front, the image shades blend with those used in the frame, thus allowing this entire image to be one of reverence. For this reason I chose to do minimal stitching and embellishing in these center columns.

- ❖ **For the Arms:** I did a triple-stitch at all the borders and left the flesh area unstitched in its entirety. Figure 10k is an illustration of two of these columns with the triple-stitching. This photo was made after the quilt had been finished, and the "Adam" columns were folded flat.

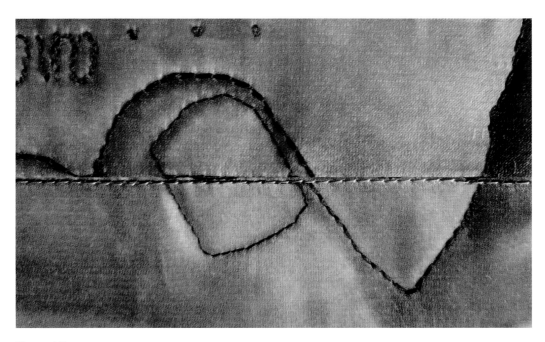

Figure 10k.

- ❖ **For the Edges of All Center Columns:** I used blanket stitches to tack down the long lines to give extra support and prevent puckering. I chose a stitch resident in my sewing machine (#1329, a simple blanket stitch in the Bernina 830), and I changed the stitch length to 4 and the width to 3. The width should be adjusted according to the amount of unstitched space that remains on each side of the central decorative stitch for each column. Figure 10l is an example that shows how the height of the stitch may vary according to what it borders. (Practically all of this stitching, though, was done at a uniform height.)

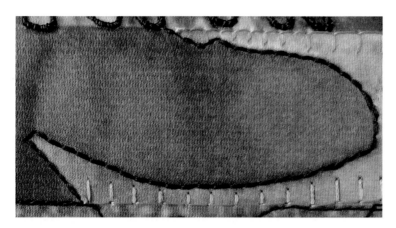

Figure 10l.

Side Notes/Tips:

❖ Keep in mind that only a small portion of the original painting (*The Creation of Adam*) is used in this quilt. This was an intentional choice because the chosen portion is frequently seen as a representation of the entire painting.

❖ For quilters who enjoy tinkering with trapunto, the flesh portions in these columns could have that effect applied to them. Although that would be tedious, it is certainly possible. The "slit the back fabric and tuck in extra batting" method might work best to attain the trapunto effect in this case.

❖ Another good stitch that can be substituted for the blanket stitch is #321, a modified cross stitch. I also used stitch #678 to fill "in between" the semicircles used for some of the column decorative stitching.

❖ Now spread out your long stitched piece and examine it in its entirety to see if there are any additional stitches needed or if you should use your craft ink pens for "touch-ups." After the folds are stitched (in the next step), it might not be possible to make some of these corrections.

❖ As you can see from all the other sections, the sky is the limit regarding what can be stitched inside the columns, if you choose to stitch anything at all. As you stitch, don't be distressed if your fabric wants to curl or pucker. That should be expected. Also, the back side of this fabric will not be very attractive. It will be covered later (no choice), so don't get concerned with its appearance.

Section Summary:

You are free to choose whether to stitch or not stitch in the narrow columns of your quilt. The information in chapters 6-10 are just detailed suggestions for your stitching. The bottom line is that you may select whatever straight, decorative, free-motion, or creative stitching that you would like. After all, it's your quilt!

Chapter 11

Sewing the Column Pleats

Up to this point you might be wondering if this is really going to become a quilt at all. You may be looking at your vast array of stitches and thinking that this just isn't going to work. However, this is where the fun actually starts!

To begin the process of making the long pleats, flip over the fabric sandwich and place it flat on a work area so the wrong side is up. Draw straight lines from the top to the bottom of the wrong side in the position where the seams will be stitched. Take care to make sure these top and bottom lines are exactly parallel and that they are within the fabric design. Also check to make sure the horizontal lines you draw will be exactly perpendicular to the column lines. If these lines were drawn on the front of the piece, it would look like Figure 11a.

Figure 11a.

Don't draw the lines on the front. The above figure is given only to show that the lines should be completely inside the image area that has been stitched. Notice how some of the design will now be included in the seam allowance and later turned under. Now flip everything over and draw these two lines on the wrong side of the fabric.

Use a large gridded ruler if you have one, or butt together two of your largest rulers to help ensure that your lines will be both straight and parallel with each other. While you are positioning the ruler(s), double-check to make sure the stitched column lines are perpendicular to the line you are drawing. Feel free to use a ball point pen here because these drawn lines will be hidden. Your piece should be similar to Figure 11b.

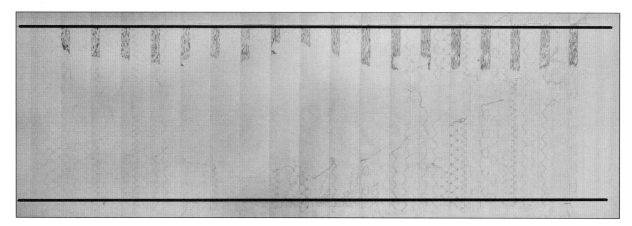

Figure 11b.

The red color is used in Figure 11b to prevent any confusion with the black stitching visible on the back. Trim away any outer edges and thread tails that are more than about ⅝" away from the drawn stitching lines.

Leave the fabric with the wrong side still up, and focus only on one long "peak/column" at a time. Begin at the left side, and pinch together the first two columns that will be forming the first pleat. On the top of this pinched section will be the stitched column line you sewed much earlier (described in Chapter 5). Hold this firmly where you have drawn the line. Your "pinch" makes a fold that will be the reverse of the later pleat and it will look like Figure 11c. Figure 11d provides additional explanatory information for the same image.

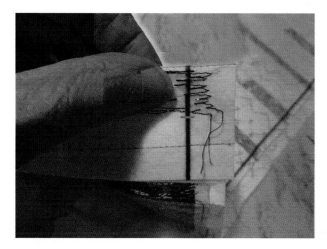

Figure 11c.

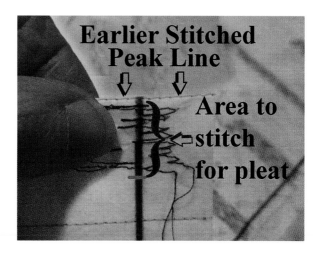

Figure 11d.

To ensure that this stitching will be in the right place, I always stick a straight pin through the two pieces where the stitching will end (at the bottom of the brackets in Figure 11d). This is shown in Figure 11e. With this pin held in place, peek underneath to make sure that's where the stitching should be. (The two column sections should "kiss" each other, as shown in Figure 11f.) If not, then move it around a bit to make it work. For cotton fabrics, these two column lines almost always abut perfectly. For silks and satin blends, I typically do lots and lots of adjusting.

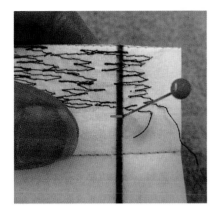

Figure 11e.

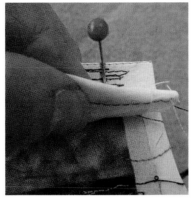

Figure 11f.

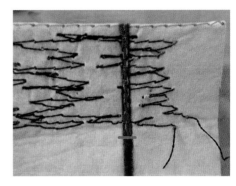

Figure 11g.

After you have the end carefully positioned, pin it place. Stitch just this end (where the bracket is shown earlier). Stitch your exact column width. (Refer to the bottom of the page for an easy, no-math way to accomplish this.) Back-stitch both at the top of the pleat and again at the bottom (to ensure it won't rip out when you turn it). Just to be on the safe side, I actually stitch this row four times—two full lengths in each direction. The red "stitches" in Figure 11g show where it has been stitched with back-stitching. Notice the stitching stopped at the blue marked line that indicated the column width. (Note: The color red was Photoshopped into this image for emphasis only; the actual threads in the real quilt were a light beige.)

After you stitch it, peek inside again to make sure it looks the way you want it. At this point, workshoppers want to know where the blue stitching line came from and how to figure just how far to stitch this column (since you can't see the column divisions from the backside). Well, there is a math way to determine this (which most of us want to avoid), but here it is: Stitch your exact column width (if you have made 1" columns, then stitch exactly 1"; if you made ½" columns, then stitch ½"columns.

Now for the easy no-math way to stitch the exact column width: First stick a pin from the right side of the fabric exactly where the two columns divide. (See Figure 11h.) Flip the fabric over (Figure 11i), and mark the exact spot where the pin has penetrated through to the other side. The blue dot in Figure 11i shows where to mark the end of the stitching line. In this manner, there is no math involved and it's very easy to do! You could actually have .87043-inch column widths and it would not matter!

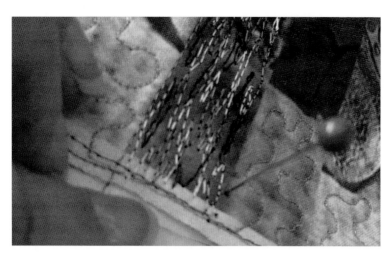

Figure 11h.

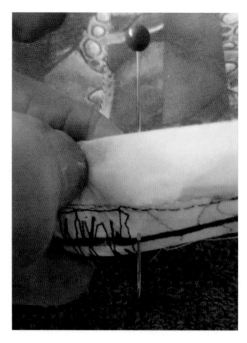

Figure 11i.

Side Notes/Tips:

❖ This is likely the most important stitching you'll be doing on this entire project, so wait until you are relaxed and not in a hurry to finish. These folds can be a bit tricky if there are differences in stitch density in the columns, but you'll get the hang of it quickly and become a pro at scooching any area that might have become a bit uneven. After the first two or three columns, it will go more quickly.

❖ Some quilters who make these 3-N-1 wall quilts will actually press the columns in the reverse before they stitch the ends. That actually is a good idea because it can prevent any accidental curving of the long columns. To do this, just use your iron after you pin both ends of the column (before you stitch the ends). Of course you'll be pressing the column crease in the opposite direction of its final destination, but the original crease will press out easily. This step is optional.

❖ Before you stitch the column edges, push any thread tails (from the column stitchings) through the outer ends so they will be caught in this pleat stitching and won't be visible later.

❖ I used a neutral thread for this sewing (Isacord #0722).

Important: Before turning these stitched column edges inside out, clip a V-shaped section away from the top outer edge of the stitched section, as shown in Figure 11j. Then clip a diagonal line, exactly up to the spot where the stitching ended, as shown in Figure 11k. Be sure to clip very carefully, getting as close to your stitching as possible without cutting those threads.

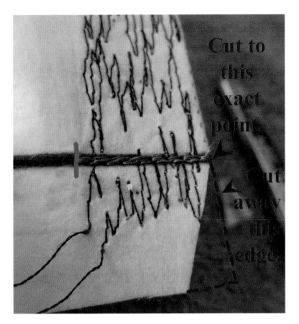

Figure 11j.

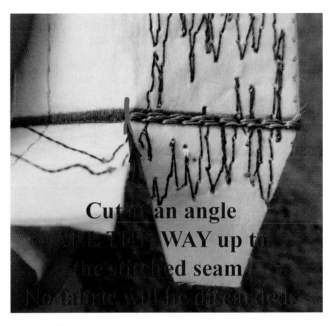

Figure 11k.

The next step is to flip this pleat back into its right-side-out position. I use a wooden Point Turner for this. Don't use a metal one because you don't want to risk having the now-narrow edges of the point to accidentally poke through. The fabric that formed the "V" will now be tucked inside and will never be seen. If you see any puckering after you have turned the pleat, this indicates that you didn't clip closely enough. Go back and very carefully snip another thread or two. Figures 11l and 11m show the two different sides of this same pleat after it was turned right side out.

Figure 11l.

Figure 11m.

Now do the same for the other end of the same column. Before proceeding to the next columns, carefully fold the entire length of this pleat and straight-stitch it through the two indicated column separation lines, as shown in Figure 11n. If you have the fabric aligned properly, these column lines in the fabric design become your exact stitch lines. Do 2-3 backstitches at both the beginning and end of each of these rows.

Figure 11n.

Notice that when you finish stitching several of these right/left columns together, the extensions of the center columns protrude and are quite unsightly. However, don't trim them. Ignore them for now, and do not try to tidy them up—they will serve a very important purpose later. They now overlap into the new extended seam allowance, and you will want them to look something like the image in Figure 11o. Notice how the "V" wedges cross over each other. Don't try to eliminate these overlapping fabric bits.

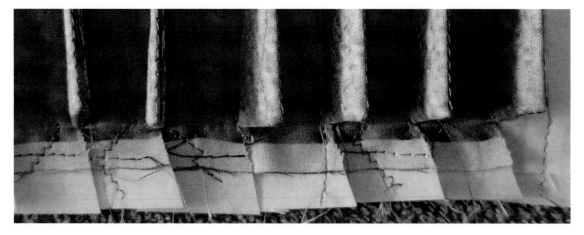

Figure 11o.

Side Notes/Tips:

❖ Don't be tempted to chain-stitch all the pleat edges on the entire quilt before flipping and stitching each of the long columns. Doing so will make the section totally unmanageable! Trust me on this one!

❖ Before stitching these column lines, double-check to make sure the top stitches and the bobbin stitching will hit at the same column separation line. This can be accomplished by placing a straight pin through the two butted-together pieces of the folded fabric to see where the straight-stitching will hit. Adjust as necessary (and that might be often).

❖ Be sure to push the center column fabric extensions to the outside before stitching the column lines. Sometimes they want to sneak under your next pleat, which means you would have some stitch-removal to do.

❖ If you have lots of dense stitching in some areas that need to crease, lightly mist the fabric on that line. The dampness will coax the fabric to bend in the desired direction.

❖ Stitch these long columns slowly. However speedy you've become with your stippling, go slowly down these columns. It is very important that these lines be straight and that the folds occur exactly where they should, or the final piece may be disappointing.

❖ There may be lots of pin-poking to get the above accomplished. A pin or two might just prick your finger, if you're not careful, blood dots can decorate your soon-to-be-finished quilt. Keep some small band aids handy, just in case.

After stitching each separate column, press on both the right and wrong sides (with a dry iron) in each direction before proceeding to the next column. Begin pressing on the wrong side in order to avoid some automatic tucks that can occur from right-side pressing. You are now beginning to tame these columns to behave as you wish for the future—which is to **stand up straight**. By pressing each column after it has been stitched, you will have a much easier time with the final pressing. When I use non-cotton fabrics, I do lots and lots of misting/dampening and pressing/coaxing at this point, and I'm later pleased that I did! Cotton fabrics, however, need practically no taming.

Continue with each of the double-column pleat sections in this manner until the entire piece is stitched into columns. Your first column will take the longest because you are learning the routine. The second column will go a bit faster. By the time you reach the fourth or fifth, you'll be chanting: pinch at the edge... poke with a pin... mark spot in blue... peek underneath... stitch the inch... clip the edges... turn inside out... push out the pokies... peek again... stitch the full column... in your sleep!

Leave the unruly outside edges as they are (for they will be resolved later). It will look something like Figure 11p or 11q.

Figure 11p.   Figure 11q.

You will later place this pleated section inside your choice of outer frame, or add a binding that conceals this entire outer edge.

The next step involves pressing these pleats. The goal will be to press each one (this time with steam, if you wish) well enough so they will behave. After you press each column in each of the two directions, the fabric threads will have been tempted and pushed to go in both directions. The columns can therefore be coaxed to bend in either direction.

Next you will square up your pleated piece if it isn't squared up automatically. One way is to dampen the piece and T-pin it to the carpet in a perfect square or rectangle. Let it dry there overnight. Should it be tempted to return to a non-square shape, stitch it around the outside edges to one or two very thick layers of interfacing. These layers can be left inside the quilt permanently, but it will resist bending. Perfection isn't the goal here. Just make sure that the piece is visually appealing.

> ### Section Summary:
>
> This chapter demonstrates how to turn your beautiful column stitching into a pleated section that will now show off the three images in your 3-N-1 quilt.

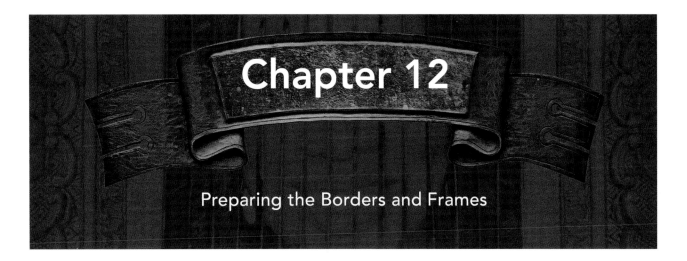

Chapter 12

Preparing the Borders and Frames

Now that you have the pleated section ready, you will need to decide whether or not you want to have a frame or any type of border around the three pleated images. Some choices are discussed below.

Easier Frames

Possibly the easiest "frame" of all is to just use an actual wooden frame. Of course you couldn't enter it into a quilt show, but it could be a gift. Figure 12a is such an example.

Figure 12a.

Another easy way is just to have no frame at all by simply turning under the outer edges and securing them to the back of the quilt with hand stitching (Figure 12b). You could sew bias binding around the edges (after trimming the outer edges to a consistent all-around width), then fold the binding to the back and hand-stitch it in place. It will still look like Figure 12b from the front, but it will have a neater appearance on the back. Another quick and easy method involves stitching a wide bias binding (as described for Figure 12b), but letting the binding remain visible as a small outer border, as shown in Figure 12c. A similar method is to stitch a solid fabric (any width) around all four sides, as shown in Figure 12d.

Figure 12b.

Figure 12c.

Figure 12d.

The most splendid method of all involves **designing your own frame** to blend with your pleated section. A frame that was specially designed for MAGICAL TOYS is shown in Figure 12e. Notice how colors in all three images are featured in the compounding borders of the frame. The patterned inner border was designed from several features of the Left Toy in the pleated insert. On the next page you can see how the finished wall quilt could look (from a front view only) after the created piece shown in Figure 12c has been stitched atop the fabric frame shown in Figure 12e. This exact frame is available for those who wish to use it. See Quilter's Note 2 in Chapter 1 for details. To prepare this outer frame, combine a top layer that will be the fabric frame, a thin middle layer of batting, and a backing as the bottom layer. Quilt these three layers together in any manner you wish. Bind the edges of the pleated section (Figure 12c), center it in the mat area, then stitch the two sections together. Finish the outside edges of the fabric frame. This method eliminates the need to make a separate backing as described in the more intricate frame section. Figure 12f shows how the above steps can be followed and an additional embellished border can be added.

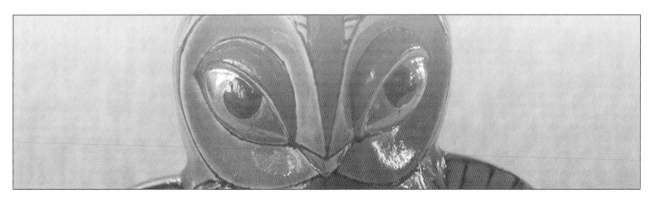

Figure 12e.

Figure 12f.

When you first look at your finished pleated section, you will surely wonder how to get the mess or tangles around the edges to eventually look smooth and professional. Although there are many ways to accomplish this, here is one suggested procedure:

❖ Use a ⅛" double-sided fabric basting tape (such as Collins Basting Tape™ or Wonder Tape™) and position that tape exactly at the edge where you will want to stitch the bias binding (single-fold). See Figure 12g. When the tape is in place, peel off the paper top. In Figure 12g, the tape has already been applied to the right edge, and it is being applied across the bottom edge in the illustration. Notice how the loose threads and the overlapping "V" sections have been smoothed out before the tape was applied, and the fabric area above the tape is smooth and clean.

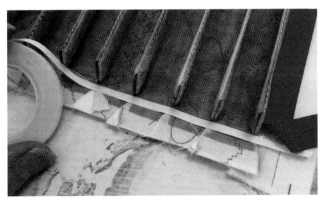

Figure 12g.

Figure 12h.

❖ Continue until the basting tape is positioned all the way around the frame. Fingerpress the bias binding strip atop one row of the positioned basting tape, easing the top of the binding to the top of the basting tape. When you get to a corner, *stop*. Very carefully *fold* the binding into a mitered corner (Figure 12h), then continue finger-pressing the next row. When you reach the starting point, clip the bias binding (leaving about a 3" tail).

❖ Now you're ready to stitch the two pieces together. If you don't care if the stitching shows, simply topstitch this at the edge nearest the pleats. If you want to hide your stitches, position your bias binding as shown in Figure 12i. *If you hadn't used the basting tape, you would need six hands to manipulate all of this and hold it in place while you stitched the binding to the pleated section.* Use your zipper foot (I use the Bernina Foot 4) and move the needle position to the farthest left slot. Open up the taped-down bias binding, and stitch on the inside crease. If you don't stitch in an exact straight line, no one will know. Stitch down as close to this crease as you can and it will be fine.

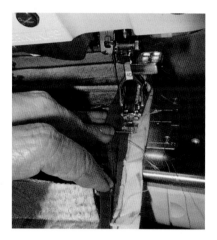

Figure 12i.

Figure 12j.

When you finish stitching all the way around, let the binding fold back on itself, and it will look like Figure 12j. Gently lift the binding and trim the excess away enough so that nothing can be seen past the binding. Hand stitch the mitered corners and the edges where the tape joins. It will look smooth and stunning! This will now look like Figure 12c, but you can stitch it atop the fabric shown in Figure 12e for a Figure 12f spectacular finish!

More Intricate Frames

As my husband and I have explored art galleries during our travels, the frames caught my attention sometimes more than the featured art pieces. As a result I have taken hundreds of photos of different frames over the years. After studying the various features of these frames through my photos, I decided to design an original frame in Photoshop that could surround the three famous art pieces in SLEEP, PRAY, SCREAM. This was quite an exciting challenge, and I feel the frame definitely enhanced the magnificent art. This specially designed frame will be used to discuss the steps on the next page.

Rationale for this intricate frame design: Unlike a whole cloth frame (such as the one shown in Figure 12e) that consists of only one fabric piece and matches only one specific set of pleated images due to color and size, this frame has two separate versatile designs. One design is for the sides (to be stitched four times, then assembled), and the other is for the optional corners (again, four times). This might seem as if it would be eight times the trouble, but it will be worth it. With this method you will also have some leeway with the exact width and length of the sides. For example, if you have a pleated insert that measures 18" x 20", this frame works—as it does for practically anything from 14" (either length or width) to about 40" (again, either length or width). Plus, with some careful maneuvering regarding sashing this frame ultimately has numerous uses.

Side Notes/Tips:

❖ The word *optional* is used for the corners because the corners can be eliminated if you have an exact square insert (or if you are happy with how the frame looks without the corners). In that case just miter your four side pieces where you want them to meet. The corners, however, do add a delightful finish to the quilt.

❖ You are welcome to use this prepared frame and corners (see Quilter's Note 2 in Chapter 1), or you may design your own frame in a similar fashion. If you order the fabric for this specially designed frame, cut each of the frame pieces into sections (the four side pieces and the four corners) and leave a very generous fabric margin whenever possible. Make sure to leave *all* of the "mat" area on the side pieces. That area can be seen at the top of Figure 12m (in the area where the text appears).

Figure 12k shows one possible look of the finished frame around an inserted pleated piece.

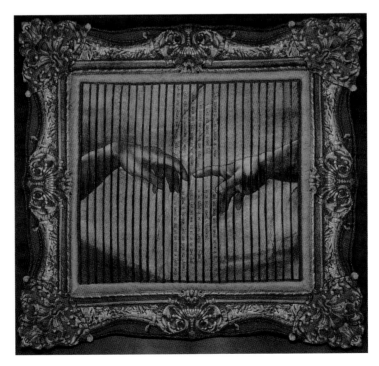

Figure 12k.

Stitching the Frame Sides

To construct the frame from the prepared fabric (or from a frame you have created in a similar manner), begin with the side. This is one design, printed four times (for each of the four sides). This single side design is shown in Figure 12l.

Figure 12l.

Now Follow These Steps:

❖ First determine the lengths of the sides that you will need to sew to accommodate your prepared 3-N-1 image insert. Add a couple inches for possible shrinkage of the side fabric in case you choose a very dense quilting design. Also think through what you want to happen in the mat areas, for example, how much matting you want to remain with the frame area. See later figures for some choices.

❖ Pin at the red-dotted vertical lines (in Figure 12m) on each end of the side panel, approximately the same distance as the length of your quilt insert. For example, if the quilt side is 24", pin two lines about 12" from each side of the center (see Figure 12m). Do not trim the remaining "leftover" fabric ends because they will be needed later.

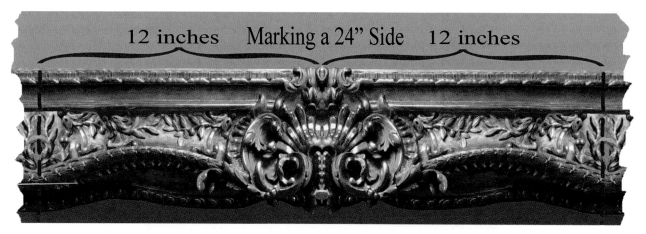

Figure 12m.

❖ Make a quilt sandwich with this frame side using two layers of batting (one thin, and an extra one of wool if you want the later faux-trapunto effect) and a backing. These extra three layers should be approximately the same size as your pinned area, with a slight extension around the edges, especially on the right and left sides. Lightly spray-baste these four pieces together in this order: frame fabric on top, wool batting, regular batting, and ending with the backing fabric.

Side Notes/Tips:

❖ The SLEEP, PRAY, SCREAM quilt needed two sides of 24" and two of 28". Therefore, the four sides were pinned accordingly.

❖ I use the extra layer of backing fabric here (even though this won't be the true back of the quilt) just because I don't like having *batting* as the bottom layer while I'm doing dense quilting. Have you ever seen a bobbin area totally clogged with "batting hair"? It's not pretty, and it is not good for your machine either. I like this method of getting rid of fabric I simply can't believe I bought! I use "ugly" or old domestic fabric I want to get rid of because this will not be what finally shows on the back.

❖ The frame will be the only part of this quilt top that will have batting. (The pleated insert has no batting.) The wool batting layer is included for frames that will have a trapunto effect. If the frame or edging you choose would not be enhanced by this technique, then use only one layer of batting that fits your chosen frame style.

❖ While I am stitching one section, I keep one of the extra identical sections nearby so I can refer to it (in case the light at my machine is blocking part of the design). This comes in handy for me.

❖ If you purchase the already prepared frame pieces, there will be an extra piece in the batch that you can use for practice. The way you decide to stitch the side or corner on your first attempt may be drastically different from your later revisions after this practice. (If your first attempt is great, then go with it! I'll be cheering you on!) Some quilters will stitch all five sections, then select the four "best" ones for their quilt.

❖ If your sewing machine has a magnifying glass attachment, this is a great time to use it. It can give a much clearer view to what you're stitching.

❖ Prepare each of these four sides in the same manner (four layers each) with the stitching lines marked or pinned.

❖ Now stitch as many straight (or gently curved) rows/sections as possible with your walking foot or dualfeed foot (I use Bernina Foot 20D). This typically gives a more professional look than with a free-motion foot. My free-motion stitches aren't very straight. Figure 12n shows a section that has been completed with the straight stitches. Notice that the stitching stopped where the area was pinned and that the outer edges aren't stitched *past* the pinned area **at this time**. More on that later.

Figure 12n.

❖ After stitching all the straight areas you see in the pattern, switch to your free-motion foot, lower the feed dogs, and proceed with quilting these four layers together as you wish. (See Chapter 13 on Sand Stitching.) I typically start near the middle because the design there is more complex and, according to many wise, mature quilters, it's always smart to start in the middle.

❖ First decide which sections of the image will be the trapunto (if you choose to have some puffed-up areas) and which sections will have the heavy stitching. Now straight-stitch around the areas you have chosen for the trapunto. I use my free-motion foot #24 because it gives me the greatest visibility. While stitching around these areas, there is no need to break your thread to go from one heavily-stitched area to another. Just do a sand stitch to travel to another area.

❖ After stitching around those areas that will remain puffed (as shown in Figure 12n), fill in all of the remaining areas with heavy sand stitches (or any other choice of stitching that you prefer). The later explanation given for the corners provides visual samples of both of these steps.

❖ Continue until your designated stitching areas, as you marked them in Figure 12m, are quilted. You will have some dangling outer-edge fabric extensions, but those will be discussed later.

❖ Stitch all four of your frame side pieces in this manner.

❖ You are now ready to join the four frame sides together. First measure the height and width you want your insert to be. Consider leaving 1-3" of the mat area for a smoother finished appearance. The more mat area there is, the less visible a slightly-less-than-square pleated insert will be. After deciding on your desired insert measurements, position the four side pieces (on the floor, a bed, or a large working area) and butt together the pieces at the corners where they will be positioned for the final quilt. One at a time, fold back the two pieces that will meet at the corner, and stitch together only the two right/top sides of the frame fabric at an angle that forms a mitered corner. Do not stitch through the two layers of batting and the backing in this stitching. Just hold (or pin) them back so they aren't included in these four corners of stitching.

❖ Turn over these pieces after you have stitched all four mitered corners, and trim the excess fabric of all four pieces in the corner mitered areas. At this point, only the top frame fabric is stitched together at the four corners, and the other three layers are loose but trimmed carefully enough so they touch ("kiss"). Flip over this entire frame section.

❖ With the right side now on the top, go back and study your stitching while they were separate pieces. The long straight (and curved) lines get close, but they don't yet meet. Now stitch them until they do meet. Do the same for the sand stitching, although if you will be attaching corners, you don't need to continue that all the way. If you don't use the corners, then complete the sand stitching until it meets. The backs of these four joined pieces will now look like Figure 12o.

Figure 12o.

❖ Flip this over to the right side and stitch around the outer edge exactly "one thread's worth" outside the edge of the frame-side design, all around the frame fabric. Stitch through all four layers. Use a bobbin thread color that can be clearly seen on the back. Stitch this perimeter line smoothly. The red line in Figure 12p shows how this stitching could be *seen from the back* although you'll be stitching on the front. Many more details for this process are given in the Corner section that follows.

Figure 12p.

❖ Set aside this frame until you complete the four corners.

Stitching the Frame Corners

Figure 12q shows the design of the piece used for these corners.

Figure 12-q.

The procedure for preparing the corners will be similar to the sides and is as follows:

❖ Make a four layer fabric sandwich and lightly spray-baste these four pieces together in this order: corner fabric on top, wool batting, and regular batting, ending with the backing fabric.

❖ Stitch in the same fashion as explained for the sides. This is done by first stitching the lines that will surround the trapunto effect sections, except for the parts around the outer edge of the design. Leave those alone for now. One enlarged, close-up stitched example is shown in Figure 12r.

Figure 12r.

❖ Follow that by sand stitching the non-trapuntoed sections. Figure 12s shows a fully completed corner and Figure 12t shows an up-close section in the same area.

Figure 12s.

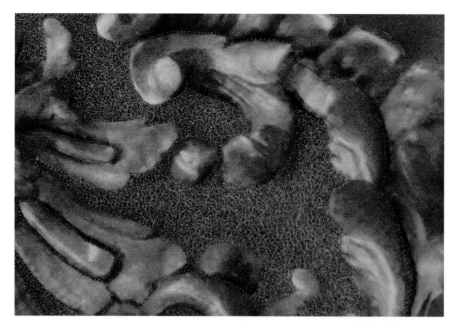

Figure 12t.

❖ After all of the quilting is complete, then stitch "one thread's worth" outside the edge, all around the corner fabric still using your free-motion foot. Stitch through all four layers. At this point make sure you use a color of bobbin thread that can be clearly seen on the back after the stitching is finished, not one that blends in with the temporary backing fabric. I used a domestic fabric, so my brown bobbin thread showed clearly, but that might not be the case with your project. Try to stitch this perimeter line smoothly. The red line in Figure 12u shows where this stitching should occur. The red line in Figure 12v shows what the stitching will look like on the back. That red stitching will serve later as your sewing guidelines.

Figure 12u.

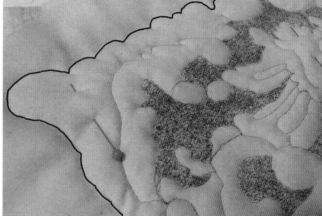

Figure 12v.

❖ Now open the layers at the outside edges and trim away the batting that extends past this outer seam, taking great care not to snip the stitching or fabric. It isn't necessary to snip extremely close— just enough to remove the bulk of the two layers of batting.

Side Notes/Tips:

❖ The red lines in Figures 12u through 12w were generated in Adobe® Photoshop® for the sake of emphasis. I didn't actually draw a red line on the fabric; the color was added to these illustrations so you could see where the stitching was intended.

❖ The purpose of stitching the red line (shown in Figure 12v) is so that when you flip over your layers, you will know exactly where to stitch.

Note: You will be making an extra quilt sandwich (of backing, batting, and a cover layer) to serve as a full back of the entire quilt. This is explained in Chapter 14. As you decide on this *permanent* backing fabric for the full quilt, keep in mind that after this fabric has been stitched and turned, several tidbits of it may peek around the edges no matter how carefully you've sewn everything together. Let that be a factor in your fabric choice. Pick something that looks very similar to the frame fabric.

❖ Pull the fabric that you have selected for that final backing unit and cut out four pieces that are slightly larger than each of these stitched corners.

❖ Place the **right side** of one of these backing pieces onto the right side of one corner. Pin these four layers together. Flip over the entire piece, and stitch **one thread's worth inside** the red stitching line that you stitched earlier. You will be able to see your earlier stitched perimeter. Stitch all the way around—leaving no opening at all. Make this stitching as smooth as possible and make sure the stitch length is **close**. Figure 12-w shows this new stitching line in blue (just a thread's-worth **inside** the red line).

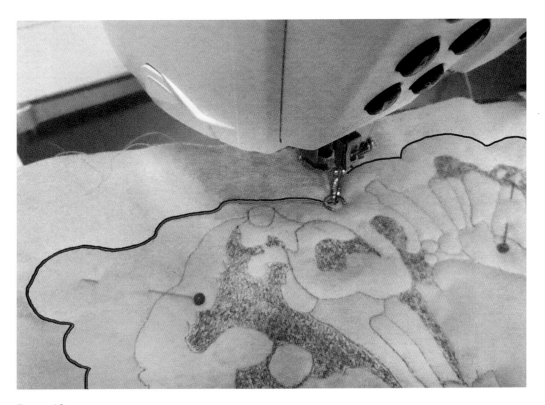

Figure 12w.

❖ Trim (very, very carefully) around this opening leaving a scant ¼" edge, as shown in Figure 12x. (Ignore the black dotted line for now.) Now clip and notch where there are "peaks" and "valleys" (using your garment-sewing knowledge). Double-check to be sure you haven't missed any valleys. If so, that would cause extra steps later. A small section of this clipping and notching can be seen in Figure 12y. You are cutting through all five layers, and the reason you are notching (in addition to clipping) is to reduce the bulk of these soon-to-be ten layers of fabric.

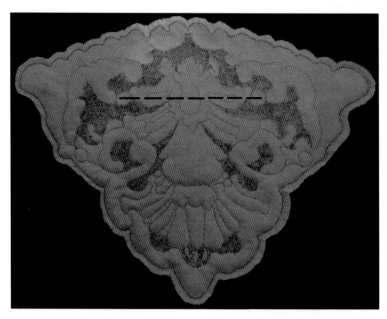

Figure 12x.

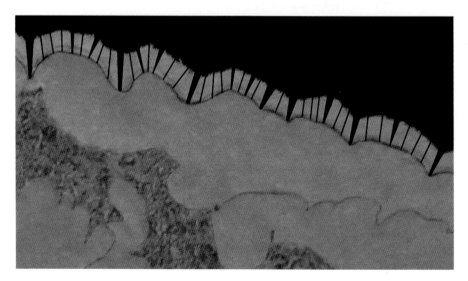

Figure 12y.

❖ In the area about 3" away from the long bias side of the *new* backing fabric only, make a 6-8" straight slit—enough so this piece can be turned. The black dotted line in Figure 12x shows the approximate position for this slit, but it will be cut *only* on the new *backing* fabric and *not* through any other layers.

❖ Turn this piece inside out through the slit, taking great care to accentuate the fabric design features at these edges. Take time and care with this, because the results can be truly smooth and professional looking. If you don't have the wooden tool called a Point Turner and Presser, it would be a great minimal investment. Sharp steel turners can damage the great work you've done so far, so be very careful with this process. If you forgot to clip an area that seems to pucker, turn it inside out again and clip it. You may leave the slit/opening as it is (because it won't be seen after the frame has been completed). Figure 12z shows what one portion of a completed corner can look like. Notice just how professional and smooth the edges look!

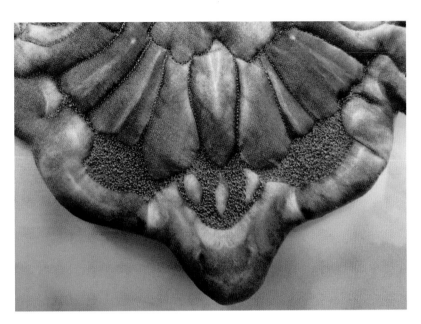

Figure 12z.

❖ Do not dismay if your completed corner has "shrunk" considerably from the original size. That always happens. Very tight stitching will draw in the fabric. This is one of the many reasons these corners and sides are stitched separately.

❖ Follow this same procedure for the remaining three corners.

❖ Set aside these finished corners for later application.

These four completed corner pieces are now independent sections of the quilt. They can be positioned and repositioned wherever you like on your quilt, at a later point.

> ### Section Summary:
> This chapter demonstrates how the four pieces of the frame sides and the four pieces of the corner units are prepared to constitute the entire outer frame that will surround the earlier-prepared pleated unit.

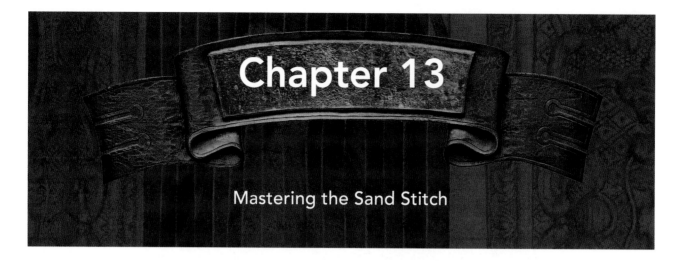

Chapter 13

Mastering the Sand Stitch

There are numerous stitching patterns that can be used in these corners and frame sides for this 3-N-1 wall quilt. You likely have some of your own favorite stitches by this point. If you do, I still encourage you to try the one explained in this chapter anyway. Who knows, it might just become your new favorite (or at least a choice for some later projects).

Fig 13a shows the dense stitching of the fabric surface. Notice the "rough wood" appearance.

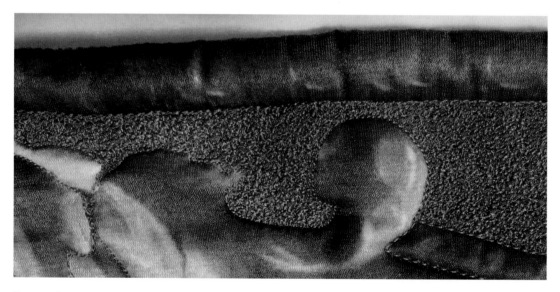

Figure 13a.

Purpose of the sand stitch:

This stitch is used to flatten the fabric in an interesting and appealing manner, especially in sections where the trapunto effect is desired in adjacent quilt sections. Can you see how the adjacent unstitched sections in Figure 13a seem to "puff up?" This is because the sand stitch can flatten some sections, leaving the batting in adjacent sections without any suppression, thus appearing larger.

Side Notes/Tips:

❖ I have always enjoyed and admired trapunto areas in quilts. I've tried every method I could find with the frames of this quilt, including the (earlier) traditional process that involved slitting the quilt backing and stuffing in extra batting. That process, however, was very difficult for the irregular sections of this fabric design representing the wood in an art frame, so I began searching for other means to accomplish this effect. After a very long exploration period, I decided on what I now call a "Sand Stitch," because the results look like a scattering of sand on a flat surface—perfect for these frames.

❖ This is a **no-fail** method. It is the absolutely the easiest tiny quilting I've ever done! With just a few minutes of practice, you can master this stitch!

❖ Suggested needle and foot: I used an Organ #80/12S Embroidery needle (larger than you might expect). I like the semi-perforations this needle makes in the fabric. I use Bernina Foot 24 (designed for free-motion quilting) with the feed dogs in the down position.

Process: Here is one suggested method for initial sand stitching practice:

❖ Prepare a small quilt sandwich (approximately 12" x 12").

❖ Straight-stitch some outer curved or straight lines to indicate mock edges or borders that will enclose later sand stitching. Refer to the samples shown on the next page.

❖ Begin on one of the outer stitched lines. Manually drop the needle any place on a border line. Begin stitching slowly in short, curvy lines. Gradually go to short rows of "skinny eights" or tiny, wavy, irregular stitches. Practice until you can get these 8's or your chosen substitute pattern to be less than a ¼" in height. Stitch these from one point of the border to an opposite border point in tiny, very uneven, and curvy rows. When you get to an opposite edge with a row of these 8's, travel slightly to one side until you are in a position to stitch another *almost* parallel row of these 8's. Continue this until you have a small section covered. The good news is that you never need to stitch in a straight line.

❖ Now stitch the same thing over the already stitched section using an angle (such as 45, 60, or 90 degrees), without any planned evenness or regularity.

❖ Before leaving the stitched section, travel back over the area and fill in any unwanted gaps. Note that in making *sand*, there will be small grains and larger grains, so everything doesn't need to be filled in completely—just enough to make the adjacent sides appear have a trapunto effect.

❖ Now take a look at your stitched section. What do you want to modify (if anything)? If so, stitch whatever you think it might need, such as an area that isn't as dense as you would like. In that case just sand stitch back to that section and "dense-it-up."

Side Notes/Tips:

❖ Keep all your stitches **very short**.

❖ Stitch at a constant speed.

❖ When stopping to reposition your hands, make sure the needle is in the needledown position before moving your hands.

❖ Never start up again without taking 1-2 tiny, close stitches before getting the fabric moving again.

❖ After you have finished one section, wiggle over to another section and do the same process. In order to do continuous quilting, travel *through* already-stitched *sand* to get to another part that needs sand stitching. Or travel along previous stitched lines until you reach the next section. Continue until all your sand stitching has been done.

❖ Keep on practicing this sand stitch until you are comfortable applying it on your projects.

See figures 13b. and 13c. for some additional sand stitched samples.

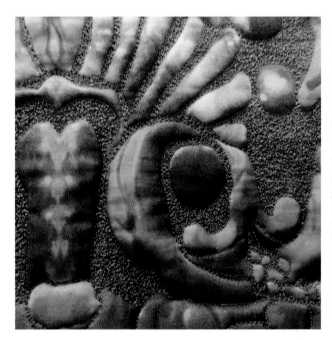

Figure 13b.

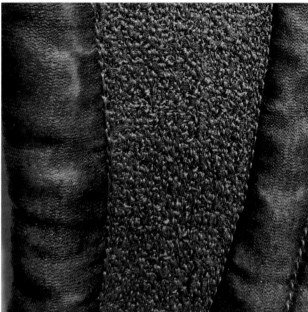

Figure 13c.

> ### Section Summary:
> This chapter describes how to use a sand stitch to create the trapunto effect in adjacent quilt sections.

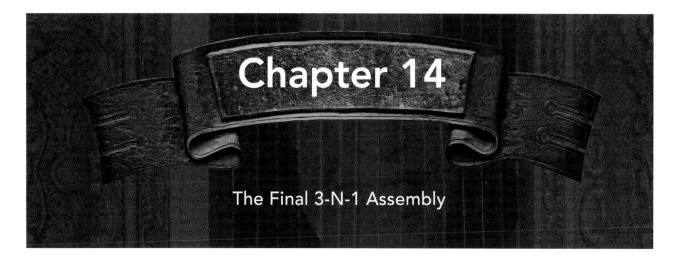

Chapter 14

The Final 3-N-1 Assembly

You are finally near the end! You have finished your pleated insert and your frame pieces are quilted. In order to hold everything together, this quilt style needs an additional separate backing (unless you choose to do one of the easier frames described in Chapter 12). To accomplish this, make a quilt sandwich (slightly larger than your prepared frame) from a neutral fabric, a thin batting, and a backing fabric. Quilt these three layers together. (The bottom layer of Figure 14a shows that separate backing section.)

Process: To assemble and complete your quilt, do the following steps:

❖ Place your pieced frame (the four sides only, not the separate corners) on top of the backing with right sides together and stitch around the outer edge exactly one thread's worth inside the red perimeter line shown in Figure 12p. See Figure 14a below, which shows the separate backing section on the bottom and the frame (wrong side up) placed atop the backing all ready to stitch together.

Figure 14a.

Figure 14b shows this same process with different fabrics.

Figure 14b.

❖ Trim the seams around the outside edges to less than a ½", and carefully clean up any curves (if you have any) in the same manner as described for the frame corners in Chapter 12. (Review figure 12y.) These steps are extremely crucial. Now turn this entire piece inside out. You will have a backing with a large "hole" in the frame on the front.

❖ Now you're ready to attach the four corners to this section by carefully stitching them together in the desired places. I used a leather needle for this section. Figure 14c shows one possibility for this stitching as indicated by the red lines. However, any way you choose to attach these corners will work, including hand-stitching.

Figure 14c.

It will now resemble the frame shown in Figure 14d. *The mat area in Figure 14d has about half of the mat area tucked underneath itself.*

Figure 14d.

At this point the new backing section and the frame are connected *only* by the stitching around the perimeter (and any stitched corner attachments). No inner lines have yet been stitched. The quilt will be further secured when the pleated insert is added.

Figure 14e.

Insert/tuck your set-aside pleated section inside the open area of the frame.

There are several choices for securing these two pieces together, such as:

Choice 1: Trim the excess frame fabric that overlaps the pleated section (at the edge of the "matting"), *leaving about a ½" all the way around for a seam allowance*. <u>Tuck under</u> this seam allowance edge of the mat fabric, as shown in Figure 14e.

Hand or machine stitch these layers together. A zipper foot will allow you to machine-stitch as close as possible to the pleats. There are several decorative stitches that work nicely for this area. See the "attaching" decorative stitches in Figure 14f (from a different quilt).

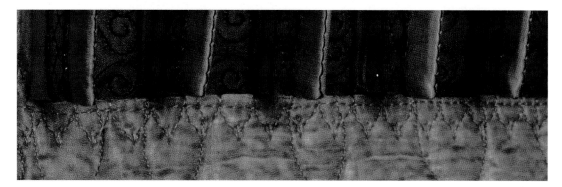

Figure 14f.

Choice 2: Topstitch a **matching narrow ribbon or a decorative trim** to secure the frame and pleated section. Figure 14g shows one possible outcome.

❖ You can now further reinforce the layers together by stitching atop any of the straight lines in the matting or frame areas. Doing so can enhance the trapunto effect even more.

Now take a look at this masterpiece and ask yourself if there is anything else you might want to do to make it look even more amazing. If so, go for it! If not, just pat yourself on the back! You are ready to stun your friends in the quilting world!

Figure 14g.

> **Section Summary:**
>
> Make a three-layer separate backing section for the entire quilt and attach it to your frame. Add the (optional) corners, insert and stitch your pleated section for a finished 3-N-1 quilt.

Bonus Chapter

The FRAME OF MIND Quilt

When I began my very first quilt with this 3-N-1 concept, I had no idea the amazing journey that this wall quilt would take. FRAME OF MIND features three famous women who have strongly influenced my life.

Figure 15a shows this quilt (with the right and left views superimposed over the center image).

Figure 15a.

With its first national appearance at the 2014 IQA Show in Houston, FRAME OF MIND won both a second place ribbon and the Viewers' Choice award. It continued to receive the Viewers' Choice in every show it has entered since (including Road to California, AQS QuiltWeek in Lancaster and Paducah). The ribbons are continuing and the journey's excitement is increasing. I will enjoy it while it lasts. In my humble opinion, that's what we should all do as we make our quilts: Enjoy the ride.

Unfortunately, while I was making the FRAME OF MIND quilt, I did not make photographs that demonstrated the process of the steps for this unusual procedure. Many were made after the quilt was finished, and they are used for this chapter's illustrations to show a few of the stitching and quilting choices. Note that these photos were all taken after the pleated section was finished and inserted into the frame section.

Thread Painting: Facial Features

The eye features (such as lashes, brows, and eye shapes) lend themselves well to thread painting. Figure 15b is one example of this.

Figure 15b.

Thread Painting: Hair

When people are featured in 3-N-1 quilts, there is the opportunity to thread paint the hair. Figure 15c shows how this was accomplished with the ends of hair strands. Figure 15d shows how different thread shades may be used for highlighting the hair.

Figure 15c.

Figure 15d.

Free-Motion Stitching: Jewelry

One woman in this quilt was wearing three strands of pearls. Figure 15e shows how this was free-motion stitched by following the pattern in the image.

Figure 15e.

Using Decorative Stitches: Clothing

Whenever clothing can be seen in the images, many fun stitching choices arise. Two different dresses in this quilt were embellished with the sewing machine's programmed stitches. Both of these dresses can be seen in Figure 15f, one in the front view and the other in the left view. The center dress has added satin-stitched scallops to appear as faux lace. The dress from the left view has solid decorative machine stitches with couched strands of thread on both sides from the decorative stitching. As an alternative, those strands could be stitched on later or even omitted.

Figure 15g shows an up-close illustration of decorative stitching in one of the dress areas.

Figure 15f.

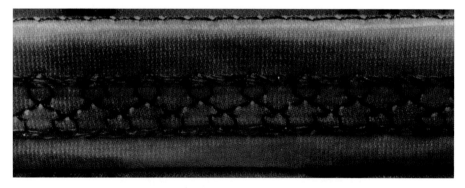

Figure 15g.

Using Decorative Stitches: Frame Matting and Pleated Columns

When the pleated inset is tucked into the outer frame, numerous decorative stitches can enhance the beauty of this merger. Additionally it provides the necessary stabilization of the two separate quilt sections.

Figure 15h shows one illustration of how this can be accomplished. This image also shows how the machine's decorative stitches can be used for the pleated columns in neutral areas.

Figure 15h.

Stitching the Frame

As was demonstrated in Chapter 12, anything can happen in the frame. The frame for this quilt used both free-motion stitching and decorative stitching to make the frame have a trapunto effect. One such section is shown in Figure 15i.

Figure 15i.

There are no limits regarding what can be done with your own 3-N-1 quilt! Do keep the fun and pleasure in the process.

Statement of Intent

In the development of Flora Joy's TRISPECTIVE, THE 3-N-1 QUILT, there were many considerations.

The intent was and remains to honor these three women by maintaining their features though the creation of a new, transformative work that would capture and inspire others.

In consideration of this goal, more than fifty images were used in combination, with a color change to sepia to produce the composite images for Trispective. These images should be recognized as composites and have been limited in their use to this one quilt.

Determination of the three women selected for inclusion on the quilt was based on their ability to influence and create change. Although the environment in which each lived and worked differed, their goals remained the same: to reach, to aid, to serve. It is because of their unified goals, these icons are unified on this quilt.

Jacqueline Kennedy Onassis graced us with style and class, but she made significant contributions to our world through the arts. Her ability to garner attention and create worldwide friendships made her a critical political figure without ever holding office. Use of the pronoun she is redundant, but we will add.

Mother Teresa can perhaps be defined best by the word charity. Remembered for her giving nature, she impacted our world through her dedication to those who often go unnoticed.

All three were chosen by Flora Joy because of the example they set and the incorporation of that example into her own life. The greatest of these three influences, is that of Oprah. Flora has read extensively about the start of life handed to Oprah and her rise from the ashes to become a social force. The values and ethics held by Oprah have impacted Flora, as she formulated and refined her personal values.

TRISPECTIVE, THE 3-N-1 QUILT is offered as an educational tool. Quilters may utilize this technology to create a different form of quilting by combining image. All images used for educational purposes have been used with permission and are strictly for tutorial.

Adobe® Photoshop® screenshots reprinted with permission from Adobe Systems Incorporated.

In closing, every once in a blue moon, there comes a work of art that is so transformative it requires attention from us all. The elements of reaching beyond self, aiding those in need, while maintaining the heart of a servant were all considered for this work. Flora developed her work with an artistic intent while looking into the post-modern, holistic woman. In doing so, this work reminds us that we are not one person, alone, but an amalgamation of those who have come before.

About the Author

Dr. Flora Joy graduated with honors with a Bachelor of Science degree and began teaching at age 18, just two years after high school graduation. She still holds the record for being East Tennessee State University's youngest graduate. Four years later she received a Master's Degree in Reading and was selected Teacher of the Year for the State of Tennessee. She taught full-time from 1963-2000 from elementary through college levels. In 2000, she received the Lifetime Achievement Award from the National Storytelling Network. From August of 2000 through May of 2004 she served as a Senior Faculty Affiliate in the Department of Curriculum and Instruction. She then segued into full retirement from teaching in May of 2004. In 2011 she was inducted into the ETSU Alumni Hall of Fame for the College of Education. She has written over 30 books, published innumerable journal articles, and her professional presentations have exceeded a thousand. In April of 2013, the campus of East Tennessee State University named a new street after her, "Flora Joy Lane." This is an honor she deeply cherishes!

She has made numerous presentations with her fabric arts and quilting productions. Some of her works have been showcased at national and international quilt shows, such as IQA at Houston, Road to California, AQS QuiltWeek Lancaster, and Paducah, the National Quilt Show, the Quilt and Fiber Arts Festival, the Mid-Atlantic Quilt Festival, the Asheville Quilt Show, Hands-On Museum, the Carroll Reece Museum, Tennessee Quilt Fest, the Blue Ridge Quilt Guild, and the Johnson City Arts Council. She has won dozens of ribbons, including five Viewers' Choice awards at Houston (the International Quilt Show), Road to California, and the AQS QuiltWeek Shows in Lancaster and Paducah. Her passion is not only making art quilts, but in the discovery of different or unique quilting concepts and techniques. She would definitely rather sew than to eat or sleep, and that's saying a lot!

MORE AQS BOOKS

This is only a small selection of the books available from the American Quilter's Society. AQS books are known worldwide for timely topics, clear writing, beautiful color photos, and accurate illustrations and patterns. The following books are available from your local bookseller, quilt shop, or public library.

#7265

#1692

#5730

#7262

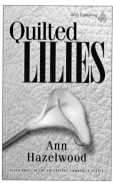

#1697

#1693

#1698

#7274

#1696

Look for these books nationally. **Call** or **visit** our website at

www.americanquilter.com

1-800-626-5420